# Penny in My Shoe

By Lone E. Janson
Edited by Anne M. Darrow

# Penny in My Shoe

ISBN: 9-781578-333561

First Edition    10 9 8 7 6 5 4 3 2 1

Printed September 2006

Book design: Mike Larsen, Todd Communications
Cover design: Anne Darrow

Published by
Todd Communications
203 W. 15th Ave. Suite 102
Anchorage, Alaska 99501
Tel. (907) 274-8633
Fax (907) 276-6858
e-mail: sales@toddcom.com
WWW.ALASKABOOKSANDCALENDARS.COM

with other offices in Ketchikan, Juneau, Fairbanks and Nome, Alaska

Printed in the United States of America.

# Foreword

In 1947 a young 20-year-old woman sat down with her little Underwood typewriter and began to write the story of her first two chaotic years in Alaska. Two published books and uncounted articles and news columns later, after nearly sixty years of writing, she returned to the telling of this story. From a "sourdough" point of view, she has seen many changes in her sixty years of living and writing and taking part in politics in Alaska.

The crazy cheechako girl who packed her "bindle" on a boat and set out to discover adventure in Territorial Alaska experienced the opening of the Alcan Highway, met and talked to such characters as the famous "Ma" Pullen of Skagway, was fired by the First Lady of Alaska, worked on the White Pass & Yukon Railroad, hitchhiked the Richardson Highway when it was only a dirt road, flew with bush pilot "Mudhole" Smith in the early years of Cordova Airlines, and rode over the old wagon trail above Thompson Pass. And those were only some highlights of the wonders she discovered in a new and unique pioneer country. Alaska was very different then, and the people were different as well. Alaska, in all its vast wilderness, made people come together in such a way that it was like one very large, spread-out community. It was here she found that undefined, elusive quality of life she had been seeking.

Born in Colorado, she and her brother grew up in the depression years with only their mother's support. Lone learned to be self-sufficient and always upbeat during those years of constant moving and childhood independence. By the age of 16, she was working as a waitress and living on her own. She dreamed of becoming a writer, but felt she could hardly write about adventure when she had not had any adventures she considered worthy. She determined that after she graduated from high school, she would go out and search for true Jack-London-style adventure in Alaska.

She boarded the ship to Alaska alone in Seattle in the fall of 1945 with almost nothing, without a job or friends to meet her in Alaska. At just barely over five feet tall and 100 pounds, she had a bravado few people can imagine. In the next two years, she worked whatever jobs she could find, made friends and met interesting people, traveled where adventure led her, and found a way of life that spoke to her own free spirit. Here was a new land full of adventure every day and endless writing possibility. This is her story of those two years of discovery.

Today at 76, Lone lives in the Pioneer Home and no longer writes. Forced into retirement by the early stages of Alzheimer's, it is good that she had written

*Lone E. Janson*

down her story long ago. She barely remembers those early years, but she has this book to remind her, and to share her story with those who were not lucky enough to come to Alaska in its pioneer years.

When Lone's first book *The Copper Spike* came out, she signed over one of the first editions to me, her daughter, in this way: "…for my little book orphan…" But I think that in all those years of growing up in the shadow of Mom's writing, I was more like an apprentice than an orphan, and I am honored that she entrusted the finishing of this last book to me. I have endeavored always during my editing to retain Lone's story in her own words. This book is truly Lone's book, the way she recorded it in her journals and later wrote it.

I would like to take this opportunity to thank the people who helped with the editing of this book by sharing their memories of those early years working with Lone.

A special thanks to Angie Bennett Olson, who met Lone in 1947 and traveled with her to Cordova. Together they hitchhiked the Richardson Highway, and then worked on the floating cannery outside of Cordova. Angie shared some of her own pictures and her memories, as well as pre-reading the book for accuracy. Others who have helped by sharing their memories are my own aunts, known in this book as "the Mad Hansens." In particular Mae (Hansen) Lange and her husband Fred, who sat with me and looked at the old pictures, sharing informa-tion about the people and events pictured there. Although she wasn't working with the "Mad Hansens" on the floater, I would also like to thank my Aunt Stella (Hansen) Janson, who was able to fill in some important information about Cordova, the fisheries and the people.

In addition, I want to remember herein my father, Roy L. Hansen, who took the picture of Lone on the iceberg, and who undoubtedly encouraged her writing when she first began. And last but far from least, I want to remember also my stepfather, Richard Janson Jr., who played a *major* role in Lone's writing career and life in Alaska.

In addition, I want to thank anyone who assisted my mother while she was writing the first draft of this book. They will know who they are, and that Lone appreciated their help.

Here it is, Mom, your story. Thanks for sharing your memories of a wonderful frontier Alaska. And thanks for making us, your children and grandchildren, Alaskans.

Anne Marie Hansen Darrow

# TABLE OF CONTENTS

*Lone E. Janson*

# Chapter One

## NORTH TO ADVENTURE

### August 1945

"And as the last smoke from the gunshots cleared away, both the brave town marshal and the infamous badman of Skagway, 'Soapy Smith,' lay dead."

Not a very good book, but it was a true tale at least, and fairly typical of the stuff I was reading about Alaska back in the 1940s while we waited for the end of World War II.

I heard the tales of Soapy Smith and "Ma" Pullen of Skagway; of the famous Canadian railroad builder Michael J. Heney; of "Cap" Lathrop, Alaska's one and only millionaire; and of the far Aleutian Islands, so recently wrested back from the Japanese. I soaked up Robert Service with his Iceworm Cocktails and "Cremation of Sam McGee," and Jack London's macho tales of danger and death along the Yukon trails. In those days there weren't as many books about Alaska, and they were almost without exception filled with misinformation.

Even textbooks weren't exempt. One of my earliest memories is a page in a school textbook with a dog sled, Eskimos and Northern Lights. Underneath was the caption "JUNEAU." The inference that Juneau was a land of ice and snow and dog sleds stayed with me for a long time, until I actually saw Juneau with its warm rainy climate, its sparkling blue waters, and its green, verdant beauty. But that had been a school textbook! The epitome of accuracy, or at least it should have been.

Oh, those books on Alaska! All myth and no substance, but since it was the myth I wanted anyway, I didn't care. It was 1945, World War II was almost over, and I had Alaska Fever. All through the wartime years while I finished high school and worked in war-related jobs, I squeezed every nickel "till the buffalo bellowed." I worked at various jobs, but mostly restaurants, and most of the tips went into "War Bonds," which I saved for that long-dreamed-of trip to Alaska.

Most of my classmates just turning 18 years old were waiting for the men to come home for marriages and families. But that wasn't my dream. I yearned only for that far north frontier.

*Eighteen-year-old Lone, just before she left for Alaska.*

I graduated from high school in the spring, and went to Seattle to be closer to the Alaska Steamship Company, which I knew provided transportation to Alaska.

With the end of World War II, I was ready to set off.

I had the feeling that if I didn't get onto the next ship to sail north, I'd never get another chance. The thought nibbled around in my mind that if I didn't go NOW, I'd never be able to. All of my friends were getting married, and while I wished them all the best, I knew it was definitely not for me!

I worked the "graveyard shift" at that time, and as I walked home one night, I saw the newspaper headline at the newsstand: "ATOMIC BOMB"!

I knew that the war would very soon be over. The very next day I went to the Alaska Steamship Company office in Seattle.

"I want a ticket to Alaska," I told the man behind the counter.

"Yes, miss," said the ticket clerk. "What city?"

My jaw dropped. In all my reading and planning, I hadn't really thought about that. I just wanted to go to Alaska!

I stalled. "Well, I don't know anybody up there, and I suppose one place is as good as another," and since that answer was obviously no help, I looked again at the big map on the wall.

Suddenly my mind was full of the gun smoke of another era. Of course I knew where I wanted to go. Soapy Smith, Ma Pullen, and the White Pass Trail!

"Skagway," I said, and the thing was done.

Only Canadian ships went to Skagway, because the White Pass & Yukon Railroad, which led north from Skagway to Whitehorse in the Yukon Territory was half-Canadian. It had been built by a Canadian, Michael J. Heney, during the Klondike Gold Rush. I booked passage on a Canadian Pacific liner, *Princess Louise*.

I had a week before the ship sailed so I went down to Vancouver, Washington, to visit my mother and collect what luggage I would have to take. I had to carry it all by myself, so I took only what was absolutely necessary—one small suitcase and a purse over my shoulder.

My mother gave me a penny and said, "When traveling, you should always carry a penny in your shoe for luck." She put that penny in my shoe herself that day.

*Lone E. Janson*

Finally, in late August 1945, the day came to get on a bus to Seattle. With that penny tucked under the liner in my shoe, I waved goodbye to Mom and happily boarded the bus for Seattle.

I found a seat right up front next to the driver where I had an unlimited view of the world I was setting out to see. I watched the sun blaze a shimmering path of gold across the water of the Columbia River. It was like an omen; I knew I was following a golden pathway to adventure.

I couldn't have picked a better place for the pursuit of adventure than Alaska in the aftermath of World War II back in 1945. Throughout the country there was a feeling of release, of new beginnings.

The War was all but over. I was eighteen and I was headed north to Alaska. I felt confident because I knew I was a good waitress. It is the best trade for an adventurer because, on account of the tips, you have some money in your pocket the very first day you start a new job. No matter how broke you are when you start, the very first shift gives you a few "sheckles" to get through till payday. They feed you too.

I felt around in my purse and took out the small jar I had with all my tip money for the last week I worked. Maybe $25 or $30 dollars in that small jar. In those days, that would buy a lot of food and accommodations. In my coin purse was $2, and I had one un-cashed paycheck for $35, my salary for the last six-day week. That and my small horde of War Bonds was my total fortune when I started for Alaska. And of course, there was the penny in my shoe.

I had bought my ticket in advance. I was gloriously happy, as I was on my way north to adventure!

Unfortunately, adventure is not always very much fun when it is happening.

When I got off the bus in Seattle, the first blow struck. I climbed into a cab and began rummaging in my purse for the small change jar.

It was gone!

I jumped from the cab and ran into the bus station, leaving an astonished cabbie staring open-mouthed after me.

The bus wasn't there. It had gone on. I stared at the place where it had been with a sick feeling.

I sat down on a bench and fought back the tears. It would not do to begin my brave new round-the-world adventure by crying. There was a lump in my throat so big I could scarcely breathe as I sat there and considered the situation.

What to do next? I had two dollars in my purse and an un-cashed paycheck. I could use the cash to get through the night, but I might need it when I landed in Alaska. The boat would sail at 5 a.m. and I was miles from the dock. Once I got on the boat my meals would be paid for until I landed in Skagway, but there was still the rest of this day, tonight, and getting to the dock.

One thing was certain: it was best to make that two bucks last as long as possible. I remembered the YWCA in Seattle. It was clean, quiet and inexpensive—and about twelve blocks away. But if they would let me pay for my room later, well, it was worth a try.

I picked up my suitcase and began the long walk to the "Y." Oh, that suitcase was heavy, and twelve blocks is an amazingly long walk when I had planned on a nice comfy trip by cab to a nice hotel near the dock. Wasn't it Robert Burns who talked of the "best-laid plans of mice and men"?

But eventually I got there, and my two bucks were still intact. After a brief negotiation, they agreed to let me stay overnight on credit. The room rent was about 60 cents, but out of only two dollars it was a big chunk. I decided against spending money on dinner; I could eat on the boat next day. I turned in for a fitful sleep.

It was the gray, dismal hour just before dawn when I started walking. I knew the steamship dock was three or four miles away, so I wanted an early start. The first mile or so wasn't too bad. The suitcase seemed light enough when I started out, but it soon felt like it weighed a ton. I had to keep shifting it from one hand to the other. No matter which hand it was carried in, I was off balance. The penny in my shoe chafed, and I was hungry. I decided I'd blow a nickel on a cup of coffee, but I never once passed a cafe that was open.

By the second mile I was feeling thoroughly sorry for myself. I was tired, and hunger adds enormously to misery. Even the prospect of sailing to Alaska was losing its bright promise. And the penny in my shoe hurt—my good luck charm. I promised myself I'd buy a pair of "penny loafers" as soon as I could. Penny loafers were popular in those days; they had a slot in the top just right for tucking in a penny. But I refused to take the penny out of my shoe. I was still on my way to Alaska, after all.

*Lone E. Janson*

I must have had about eight blocks to go when a man came up behind me. "May I help you with that suitcase?" he asked.

I was so very grateful and gladly surrendered the lopsided burden to him. He was a gentle person, willing to listen to my catalog of grief. I poured out my tale of woe, and I have never been one to understate the case. He listened patiently, making sympathetic noises in all the right places. He never once told me I was crazy to be going off to Alaska with only two dollars in my pocket. He seemed an absolute saint, a broad shoulder to cry on in lieu of breakfast.

But at last the dock came in sight. We walked up to the ship, and he handed my suitcase back to me. He wished me luck and Bon Voyage, and walked off.

It was only then that I noticed he had only one arm.

A wave of shame washed over me. Wasn't there a story about the man who wept because he had no shoes until he met a man who had no feet? I had been so sorry for myself, when I had everything in the world to be grateful for. There was nothing I could say or do; the man was gone. My feelings were all mixed up at the moment.

I turned and looked up at the *Princess Louise*. The bow soared proudly above my head, sleek and black, with the white lettering of the name across the top. Above that I could see cleats and hawsers and other fascinatingly nautical things. My heart leapt in anticipation. How very, very lucky I was! I was on my way to Alaska and adventure on a genuine cruise ship!

Suddenly my feet didn't hurt, I wasn't hungry, and I wasn't tired. I was just overwhelmingly happy!

I picked up my suitcase and walked up the gangplank.

# Chapter Two

## IT'S "TONI" IN ALASKA

### August 1945

I lugged my heavy suitcase up the gangplank, and was shown to a "stateroom." It was not exactly "stately," but to me it was the most wonderful tiny cubicle in the world. I was on my way to Alaska in this stateroom! It boasted just two single bunks, one above the other, and a space alongside about three feet wide. There was a single window at the end of the room. Under it was a small table where I set up my suitcase.

The ship was preparing to sail. With only a brief survey of these Spartan quarters, I laid claim to the upper bunk by throwing some clothes on it. I have always liked the upper bunk; to me it was something like reaching for the stars.

I didn't want to miss anything on deck so I dashed out to watch the departure.

There were no cheering crowds on the Seattle dock that day. There were only a few last minute well wishers scurrying to get off the ship before the gangplank was pulled, the throaty boom of the whistle, and the pulsating throb of engines getting under way.

I felt a shiver of excitement as I watched the longshoremen slip the hawsers from the bollards (I'd been reading a lot about sailing ships recently so I knew a few nautical terms).

I felt the vibration of engines as we pulled away from the Seattle wharf. In three days I'd be in Skagway! In Alaska!

I watched Seattle fade away in the distance.

Then I turned to explore the ship and learn my way around the various decks. People were friendly and it was easy to get acquainted. No one seemed the least perturbed by this brash young girl traveling alone to Alaska in search of adventure. They all seemed to accept it as quite the normal thing.

During my tour of the decks I discovered an immense and very detailed chart of our route mounted on the wall near the purser's office. I could follow every landmark—every buoy, rock, and point of land on

*Lone E. Janson*

the entire trip north, with the possible exception of the seagulls.

As I stood there tracing the myriad islands we would sail past, a redheaded woman came up and joined me. She was rather tall, not really much more than me, but she looked tall to me.

She said "Hi! Everyone calls me 'Red,' what's your moniker?"

I hesitated.

My given name was Lone (pronounced "Loney"). All through high school my classmates had called me "Loney-Baloney" and "Loony" and such, so now I decided that my Alaskan name was going to be different.

"My name is 'Toni'," I said.

From that day forward I became "Toni" in Alaska, and even though I wrote under my given name, it worked. In one fell swoop I had become a different person!

It occurred to me that maybe she also went under the nickname of "Red" for similar reasons. Nicknames were everywhere. I had already read about "Soapy Smith," "Klondike Kate," and others. I wanted to be like that. Not a "Loney Baloney"!

Red had a loud voice and disheveled red hair; I didn't know what to think of her. But I liked her right off. She radiated confidence, courage, and an experienced knowledge of Alaska. She had an open, hearty style about her; she was the kind of person I had always wanted to be. She was a "character"!

She launched into a story of each of the islands on that map with a little catalog of geography and history, generously spiced with offbeat humor. When she laughed, it was booming and hearty and rattled the windows.

She told me that everything outside of Alaska was called "Down Below" or "Outside." She had a little chant about the three sides of Alaska: "Inside, Outside, and Morningside!"

Morningside was a place down in Washington where our "slipped disks" were sent. Red said, "We never call them crazy; after all, any one of us might be next!"

Aside from her booming humor, she was an incredible fund of Alaskana, stuff that you could never find in any book, things that were important to Alaskans in those days.

The first thing she told me was "Never call this a 'ship'! It is always a 'boat.' I don't know why, but in Alaska it's never called a 'ship,' no matter how big it is.

"That would have marked you immediately as a 'Cheechako,' a newcomer.

"What you need to understand is that the whole culture of Alaska is based on boats like this one. Every newcomer to Alaska, every necessity—food, medicines, luxuries, all mail and freight—in fact, everything, comes to Alaska by boat!

"You'll learn a lot of new expressions, like 'steerage.' That's the super-cheap, non-luxury travel below decks, somewhere near the bilge. And 'blue ticket'—passage given to the most undesirable incorrigibles—a one-way ticket out of Alaska, no returns!"

Red was on a roll now: "Even the bums in Alaska are a better class of bums because at least they had to have the price of steerage fare!

"And of course," Red went on, "I understand that the famous 'Glacier Pilot,' Bob Reeve, arrived as a 'guest of Alaska Steam'! That means he stowed away!"

Red obviously found this very funny and her laughter was contagious. I wasn't sure who Bob Reeve was, but I laughed anyway. I was eagerly soaking up all these great sourdough tales.

"Every time a boat comes to an Alaskan port, it's like Christmas!" Red said. "Even if it comes in at 2 a.m., you'll see crowds of people on the dock waiting to greet their friends from the 'Outside,' or waiting to longshore, or watching to see old friends passing through with new wives, husbands, or babies.

"We have a saying: Alaska is like a Dickens novel, everyone you meet, you will meet again!"

I was to find out later that "Boat Day" was a grand way to keep up with the gossip. After all, Alaska was a huge country but a very small town, so to speak. The entire population of this huge Territory would not have filled a modest city back then. Everyone came and went by boat, so of course, everyone tried to meet the boat to see old friends.

Red turned more contemplative then, and seemed to have important things to tell this cheechako.

"But it's more than that when the only mail you get arrives once of week, or once a month, or in some places only once a year. The boat brings fresh fruit and vegetables, and fresh meat—frozen, of course.

*Lone E. Janson*

These things are luxuries you only enjoy on 'boat day.' In fact, the arrival of a boat is the single most important recurring event in Alaska.

"It also makes Alaska extremely vulnerable. A steamship strike can cripple the entire Territory in ways you can't imagine, Toni. They had an Alaska Steamship strike back in the '30s that staggered Alaska. The grocery stores had nothing to sell. We were out digging clams and taking seagull eggs to eat—anything we could scrounge up! And when someone in the town bagged a big prize like a moose, they cut it up and gave to the elderly people first, then to the large families. A huge moose is a lot of meat, but not for a small hungry town!"

Red stopped and shook her head. "Yep, the whole culture of Alaska depends on the boats." We stood there for a few seconds in serious silence. Then Red turned to me with a twinkle in her eye.

"Besides, what would we do without the boats to bring you cheecha-kos up here for us the laugh at!" Her booming laughter lightened the mood again, as was obviously her way.

About then, Red spotted some old friends and with a quick "see ya later" was off to visit with them.

I leaned on the rail, watching the water slide around the boat's hull. "Wow," I thought, "I could never have learned so much so soon, except from an old-timer who has experienced such things."

What made Red so memorable was that she always came up laughing. I wondered if all Alaskans had such resilience.

I was determined to record all the interesting local Alaska insights Red had told me about. I dashed to my "upper stateroom" (upper bunk) to scribble it all down while it was fresh in my mind. I had to write with a very dull pencil because it was the only one I had and there was no way to sharpen it. At this point I wasn't thinking of myself as a "writer"; I was just trying to remember every moment of this great adventure!

By now we were well up the magnificent "Inside Passage" north to Alaska. The first leg of our trip had taken us up the shores of Vancouver Island where we had a quick visit to a fish cannery town called Alert Bay.

Back on the ship—I mean, "boat"—I met all sorts of people. One of them was a Fundamentalist preacher. My experience had been that such people were very strict and unbending, but I found him very open and fun to talk to. We both laid out our religious convictions, and neither of us tried to change the other. It was quite off-key; I think it was about whether or not seagulls had souls. He thought no and I thought yes. We parted as friends and the seagull question was left for God to decide.

On my tours around the decks, I met a Greek fellow who introduced himself as Mike Putsalas. He had run Greek restaurants, and he was going to Cordova to operate a cafe.

I told him I was a waitress and had worked with Greeks back home. "The Greeks are the best bosses," I said. "They're strict but fair."

Mike was pleased, of course. I knew nothing of Cordova, but it sounded like an interesting town. Of course, every Alaska town was fascinating and I wanted to see them all! I intended to work my way around to see as much as I could of Alaska.

I said, "Maybe some day I'll meet you in Cordova!" I really wasn't sure where Cordova was.

Mike chuckled and dropped the subject, but there was a twinkle in his eye. He must have suspected he would indeed see me again, true to the Alaskan adage: "Everyone you meet in Alaska, you will meet again." Alaska was like that.

I was aware that I was the youngest passenger on the boat, and everyone was trying to be pleasant to me, but there was something else going on too. It was a special friendliness to help me get oriented. I had only just turned 18, and I had used all the money and courage I had to come to this unknown country.

Alaskans picked up on those things very quickly in those days. What I didn't know about was the shortage of women. That put me into a special category!

I hadn't figured on that sort of thing. I wanted only to experience new and wonderful things about Alaska. Marriage was the very last reason for me to come to Alaska! To me, marriage meant my adventurous life was over. I wasn't ready for that!

I was leaning on the rail when a young fellow came up and struck up a conversation. His name was Ted and it was nice to talk to someone around my own age. It turned out he was bumming around Alaska too, so we spoke the same language!

"So where you headed?" he asked.

"Skagway." I said. "I'm a waitress and I hope to find a job there for a while."

Ted said, "Fairbanks for me. I plan to go to Skagway, take the train to Whitehorse, and then probably over the new 'military highway' if it's open yet."

"They're opening it to the public?"

"Well, yeah, but you would probably need a lot of identification and tell them where you were going and all that. After all, the war isn't over yet."

"Maybe I'll go down the highway later too!"

"Well, most of the people on this ship seem to be headed up on the White Pass & Yukon to hook up with the new highway. There must be something open," Ted said hopefully.

We weren't sure of the status of the military highway. There were a lot of things that we didn't know at that momentous time.

We didn't know that the very next day, the Japanese and Americans would the sign the peace treaty. Little did I know that my brother would be on the very ship on which the treaty was signed.

As we talked, a steward came around the deck chiming on an instrument, chanting, "Full sitting for Tiffin!"

Ted and I looked at each other. Almost in the same words, we said, "What the heck is 'Tiffin'?"

It turned out to be an afternoon tea or coffee and a few sweet buns or such. It was a delightful custom!

Most of the boat's passengers were bound to Whitehorse and that new highway, on the way to Fairbanks. I was staying in Skagway. I didn't have enough money to go further. Also, I wanted to meet the famous "Ma" Pullen and hear the story of Soapy Smith.

I expected to find waitress work in Skagway. Obviously, I knew nothing of that small, interesting railroad town.

Ted and I were enjoying each other's company. Everyone else was so much older.

We were walking the decks of the boat one day, savoring the sea air and sunshine when someone spotted whales. There was a general gasping as the news went around, and we all ran to the rail to see. That first whale was far off—just a glimpse of water as he blew, but it was fascinating to me! My first whale!

We saw other whales. Some of them were just cruising along enjoying themselves. Some were in small groups, some alone. One came quite close, spouting his lovely vaporous fountain. If only it could have known what delight it brought to a young girl on her first trip to Alaska!

We also saw porpoises frolicking around the bow of the boat. And once I even caught a glimpse of a bear along the shore.

Prince Rupert was our last Canadian stop. After a short visit in that last Canadian town, we were eager to see what Alaska would look like.

I knew we were getting near the Alaskan border. I was incredibly excited. It was September 1, 1945—the day I was to arrive in Alaska at last! I stood on the deck right where I could dash in easily and check the big chart against all the landmarks, to make sure I knew the exact moment.

As it turned out, the moment was crystal clear to me, because a lighthouse marked the entrance to Alaska. We sailed past a rock with this beautiful white tower on it, with its revolving light and red roof gleaming in the sun. It looked like some kind of a painting. Surely nothing in real life could look like that!

But it did, and I was in Alaska at last. Eagerly I looked forward to our first port of call, Ketchikan. I really didn't know what to expect. Would it be a "last frontier," or would it be just another big city like Seattle or Denver?

# Chapter Three

## NARROWS, GLACIERS AND SKULLS
### September 1, 1945

Ketchikan wasn't at all like Seattle or Denver. It was truly my idea of a "frontier" town with boardwalks and signs of wilderness right at the very edges of town.

The dock had been crowded with people as we pulled into port late in the afternoon, but Ted and I hardly noticed. We were in a hurry to explore. We had only three hours in this port!

There was one facet of the frontier image that surprised me: the ultra-modern, right alongside very rustic. We walked up the main street to see a neon-lit, obviously brand new and very modern soda fountain right next to a log cabin residence. There were false-front buildings like an Old West movie set, alongside ultra-new structures. This country was so new that all the newer buildings were far more modern than the general run of business buildings in Denver or Seattle.

Ted and I heard there was a little park nearby where we might see salmon going upstream to spawn, so we set out to find it.

We discovered a huge cascading stream with a bridge across where we leaned on the rail drinking in the sound and fury of the wild water below, feeling the cold spray and even colder breeze on our faces. We watched salmon leap high in the air in their mad migration upstream against that boiling current. We cried out with delight at each salmon leap. We urged the big fish on up that roaring waterfall, up the river.

If anything ever typified what I consider Alaska spirit, it was those salmon leaping and fighting against a plunging current to reach an unknown goal upstream.

Ketchikan was called the "First City" in those days because it was always the first Alaskan city seen by anyone heading north. It almost seemed too tropical for Alaska. Known as the "Banana Belt" of Alaska, its mild, rainy climate fostered a crop of such plants as lush trees, rhododendrons, and deep green lawns. I had not expected to find such warm-weather vegetation in Alaska! I loved Ketchikan, and our corny jokes about its being "North Seattle" carried no sting.

Time flew for us. Ted and I had a quick ice cream soda in the ultra-modern soda fountain that featured a concoction called the "Rain Bird."

The thirty-minute warning whistle was tooting its throaty message as we strolled back to the steamship dock. Aboard the Princess Louise, we consulted our charts and planned our next day's adventures.

We were to dock in Wrangell at about 3 a.m., followed by a sail through the Wrangell Narrows, which I was assured was a great adventure. Incredibly narrow, it wound between two islands with many, many buoys to mark the way.

At the northern end of the narrows we would dock at the town called "Little Norway"—Petersburg. Beyond that lay Juneau and then our destination: Skagway.

"Shall we go ashore at Wrangell?" Ted asked.

"At three in the morning?" I laughed. "Sure, why not?"

I woke next morning to the deep boom of the ship's whistle as we approached Wrangell. I really wanted to roll over and go back to sleep, but if I did I might miss a magnificent adventure.

It was 2:30. We would dock soon, so I stumbled sleepily up on deck to meet Ted. He stood by the rail, shivering in the chill morning, waiting as he had promised. I joined him there and we watched the approaching lights of Wrangell. It was still night, but a pale dawn shimmered in the east as we set out to see our second town.

The usual crowds were on the dock, not as many as Ketchikan, but down to meet the boat despite the heathenish hour. We walked around the quiet dusty streets, but since nothing was open and the only sign of life appeared to be at the dock where the steamer was, we soon went back to the boat and our warm beds.

The next adventure was to be when we sailed through Wrangell Narrows. For that, I wanted to be on deck "bright-eyed and bushy-tailed."

I had been told that in some places in Wrangell Narrows it was so narrow that you could almost reach out and touch the branches of trees overhanging the water.

To my surprise, the captain of the ship invited me into the bridge as his special guest to witness this interesting event. Before starting, we waited outside the Narrows for about half an hour to allow the tide to rise higher. I spent the whole time through Wrangell Narrows on the bridge of the ship with a chart in front of me, identifying every buoy and rock.

All that I had heard was true. It truly seemed as if the trees were within arms reach as we skinned through. In these narrow quarters the world was green and summery, with lush trees and thick rain forest right down to the water's edge.

But I was nowhere prepared for the sight that greeted me as we rounded the last point before Petersburg. My first glacier!

Dead ahead, the mountains on the mainland lay gleaming white in the sun, with a blue-white glacier tumbling from its cradle between two mountains. Here nature had taken two high peaks and filled the entire space between them with ice and snow! It was breathtaking, especially after the summery warmth of the passage through Wrangell Narrows.

The stops at Petersburg and Juneau were just a blur of adventures, as we made these quick stops. The old Nugget Shop on South Franklin Street in Juneau was a landmark even then. I'm sure the Red Dog Saloon must have been there, but I was too young to drink so I didn't see that one.

One Juneau landmark I remember vividly, though, was the Alaska-Juneau Gold Mine (the "A-J") clinging to the side of the steep mountain. It was no longer operating. All but strategic mineral mines were closed during World War II. Many of them never opened again,

*A.J. Mill*

including this famous gold mine.

By then, the "A-J" had not yet suffered the big fire that destroyed its historic quality; with its miles of underground tunnels and railroad, it would have been a great tourist attraction.

Ted and I took a sightseeing bus that drove past the Governor's Mansion and some of the other places around Juneau, and then took us out to view Mendenhall Glacier.

On that trip to Mendenhall Glacier, I saw a herd of dairy cows. I didn't know that in a year or so that area would become the new Juneau airport, surrounded by a thriving suburban shopping area, and the cows would be gone.

Aboard ship again, the last leg of the voyage to Skagway was the long fiord up Lynn Canal. Here the mountains seemed to move in, becoming high and forbidding. All around were the forested islands of the "Inside Passage," very close.

What a voyage it had been so far! Standing at the rail, I reflected what a wonderful experience it had been, and I almost dreaded the end of this voyage.

Aboard the ship we had formed good friendships, but when we landed, that would all change. My new friends would go on their ways and I would be alone again. I felt sadness, but since I had lived on my own for two years already, I wasn't afraid. I would make new friends.

Skagway! The dock was right at the base of a cliff, and up on the face was a rock that had been painted as a death's head, with the inscription underneath: "Soapy Smith's Skull."

A train waited on the siding nearby, puffing noisily and hissing steam, ready to take freight over the pass to Whitehorse beyond those towering mountains.

After three days' sail, I had arrived in Alaska, ready for adventure. I was in the land of Ma Pullen, the White Pass gold rush trail, and Jefferson Randolph "Soapy" Smith.

Ted and I walked down the gangplank together, headed for the famous old Pullen House. I glanced up at Soapy's skull once more, and wondered what adventures awaited me here in Alaska.

A shiver went through me, but whether it was apprehension or anticipation, I wasn't sure.

Just like Ma Pullen when she landed here forty-seven years earlier, I needed a job, and fast! I had exactly two dollars cash in my pocket.

# Chapter Four

## IT'S DOWN THE HALL

### Skagway—September, 1945

*Pullen House in Skagway. Photo by Olaf Dole*

Pullen House was a huge, beautiful, old-fashioned, rambling white house, dominated by a glassed-in sun porch, with lots of dormers and windows—more of a home than a hotel. It was one of the most famous hostelries in the Territory of Alaska. Starting from a small cabin back in the gold rush days, "Ma" had built Pullen House into a fine little hotel, enlarging and adding onto it over the years. I had read much about this plucky Alaskan woman in all those books about Alaska.

When she arrived in Alaska in 1897, Harriet Pullen was a newly widowed young woman with four children. She had never held a job in her life and needed one, when a friend urged her to go to the Klondike with the stampede. "You can get work there." she was assured. "They say even unskilled workers are in great demand along the gold rush trails."

So it was that Harriet, a tall (5'9"), red-haired beauty, found herself in the wild, raucous new tent town of Skagway with only seven dollars and no friends or acquaintances. She had left her children home with relatives until she could get settled in Alaska.

As she stood on the shore looking at the rowdy mass of humanity around her, a man came up and asked simply: "Ever cook?"

Taken aback, Harriet replied, "A little."

"You're hired. The job pays three dollars a day. We'll need supper for eighteen tonight. Follow me."

Dazed by the suddenness of it, and by what she thought to be princely wages, she followed the man to his cook tent. By evening she had bacon and beans enough for eighteen men, plus one thing never seen before in Skagway: dried-apple pies.

Ma Pullen's dried-apple pies were such a sensation that she began baking them and selling them to miners as a sideline. Within the year she had made enough money to bring her children north to join her. She also brought up her seven horses from back home.

In early Skagway, before the railroad to the interior was built, horses were at a premium. Incredible quantities of freight had to be hauled to the gold fields over "the pass." Mostly the horses were cruelly treated, so badly that the trail became known as "Dead Horse Trail."

Worried about the welfare of her horses, but needing money desperately, she began freighting over White Pass. She was the only woman ever to do so. She wouldn't allow anyone else to work her horses because of the cruelty she had seen.

In 1898, Michael J. Heney began construction of the White Pass & Yukon Railroad, finishing it as far as the summit within two years. Freighting by horse pack then fell off.

So Ma Pullen looked around for other sources of income and bought what became Pullen House, one of the most famous hotels in Alaska, with an "at home" atmosphere.

All this I knew about Ma Pullen, and I was itching to meet her.

I checked into the Pullen House and was shown to my room, down a long corridor to a sort of annex, on the second floor. It was a large room, rather Spartan, as most rooms were in those days, furnished with only a painted dresser with wooden knobs and a bed. It was plain, but it was light, clean and airy. As for other facilities, a door down at the end of the hall proclaimed simply "Toilet." No nonsense about "Men" or "Women," just "Toilet." Another door nearby bore the matter-of-fact message: "Bath." I unpacked and decided to go out to see Skagway.

As I walked down the street, men tipped their hats as they passed me. It was a surprising and delightful old custom I was not expecting. Although I knew the ten-to-one ratio of men to women had a lot to do with it, I enjoyed it immensely.

I decided to find a restaurant and see if there were any jobs. It turned out that there was only one eatery, and the boss said he had just "hired our winter waitress!" Only one cafe with one waitress in the whole town—and I wasn't it!

I saw Mike Putselas, the Greek fellow I knew from the boat. He invited me to join his party for lunch. Mike had figured out very early that I was operating on very thin money, but he never let on.

Meanwhile there was nothing I could do until the first ship went south from Skagway to Juneau. We had just been there and the prospects for work definitely looked better for me there than where I stood now! It meant cashing in one of my "War Bonds," which I didn't want to do except in dire distress. This might be one already.

The boat would not be leaving until Monday, and it was now early Friday. I figured I might as well enjoy Skagway until then. So I spent the time with Ted exploring this interesting town.

Ted and I roamed around town, soaking up the town's history and listening to stories. One of our conversations turned to the "art" of taking a bath at Pullen's hotel.

I told Ted, "You know, taking a bath in this place is somewhat like an African Safari! You have to plan carefully and make sure to take everything you'll need."

Ted chimed, "If you forget anything, you're in deep you-know-what!"

I took up the dialogue as we picked up on the off-the-cuff comedy: "You have to climb from the tub still dripping and towel off. Then you have to re-dress, and go to your room for the forgotten item..."

Ted took the next sequence: "For me, I'd be wrapped maybe in a towel, almost in the 'altogether,' hoping no one else wanted to take a bath while I was gone!"

I was cracking up by now, "And if you see someone else with a bath towel and soap, you better do a quick turn-around and get back to the bathtub before he takes it over!"

*Lone E. Janson*

Everything we did, everything we talked about, was funny and delightful. First impressions I eagerly scribbled in my journals and conveyed home to my mother by letter. I wrote her of the way people referred to the rest of the "South 48."

"It's like referring to Hell," I wrote. "No one uses the name. It's always 'Down Below' or 'Outside.' They talk of various parts of the Great Land (which is what the Alaska name means) by referring to the 'Interior' (up around Fairbanks), or the country 'to the Westward' (meaning the Aleutian Islands). I learned of cheechakos (greenhorns like myself), and sourdoughs, and several versions of how to become a sourdough. In spite of the jokes, it was generally accepted that a person had to at least endure an Alaskan winter to even be considered for acceptance into the coveted sourdough status."

We saw beautiful big flower-filled yards, and visited the graves of Soapy Smith and Frank Reid, the town marshal who killed Soapy.

We looked for the beginning of the White Pass Trail and even hiked a few miles up before returning to the cheery fireside at Pullen House for the night.

Exploring the next day, we especially enjoyed the old wooden sidewalks that resounded to our footsteps just like something out of a Western movie. As the sound of our steps took on a rhythm, Ted began a little impromptu performance:

"Here comes the villain, Rattlesnake Charlie," he said, clomping his heels on the resounding wooden planks. Clomp, clomp, clomp.

"And here comes the brave town marshal, Dapper Dan," he continued. Clomp, clomp, clomp.

"Rattlesnake says he's going to kill Dapper Dan at High Noon." Clomp, clomp, clomp.

"But Dapper Dan, he's not afraid. He wears a white hat." Clomp, clomp, clomp.

"The villain, Rattlesnake Charlie, wears a black hat, of course." Clomp, clomp, clomp.

Ted stopped walking. The clomping ceased. Silence. "The scene is set. It's 'High Noon'!

"They face each other. The tension mounts. They draw their guns and shots ring out! Dapper Dan is still standing, but that dirty Rattlesnake Charlie has bit the dust!"

We both dissolved into gales of laughter at this little charade.

Actually, there was more than a grain of truth in it, as told by the books about the notorious "Soapy." Soapy earned his nickname by placing a $5 bill in a box of soap and advertising it for sale for a dollar. Of course, when the "mark" opened the box there was no $5 bill in any of the boxes.

Soapy had come from the rip-roaring mining town of Cripple Creek, Colorado, so he was familiar with the style and temperament of such frontier towns.

Skagway was the epitome of the gold rush boomtown—just what Soapy thrived on. He and his henchmen operated wide open out of "Jefferson Smith's Parlor," where prospectors were swindled and robbed, drunks rolled, and any kind of murder or mayhem went unpunished.

But Smith had his genteel front. Ma Pullen remembered him as a man who was mild and gentle with women and children, and she said she never felt in any danger from him. He was smart enough not to bother the business folks of Skagway, knowing that they would not challenge him if they were not getting hurt.

Soapy's gang only targeted the transient gold-seekers. He maintained such a proper bearing in town that he was the Grand Marshal of the 4th of July festivities in 1898, riding grandly on a white horse at the head of the parade. Three days later he was dead, shot by town marshal Frank Reid, who also died in the fray.

Ted and I roamed around the town, and with some trepidation we peered into "Soapy Smith's Parlor," still standing in Skagway. We enjoyed the old streets, spotted the big yellow depot of the White Pass & Yukon Railroad, and watched the tiny steam locomotives chuffing up the narrow gauge track toward the high, dizzy mountains.

Looking into the old buildings, we tried to visualize the days of '98, and admired small things, like the old-fashioned doorknobs. It was after the tourist season, so most places weren't open.

But the highlight of the weekend was the rainy evening when Ted and I got back from one of our exploring forays, soaking wet, and found Ma Pullen seated in a wheel chair in the big front room before a roaring fire.

Harriet Pullen must have been well into her eighties at that time. The beauty that had been hers had faded by then, but her personality was still there. She was a plump, silver-haired woman whose voice squeaked with age.

Ted and I huddled in the warmth of the blaze, listening to her tell of the honors won by her son in World War I. Daniel Lee Pullen, Alaska's first cadet to West Point, was decorated for heroism in World War I by General Pershing.

"They called him 'the Eskimo,'" she piped. "They called anyone from Alaska an 'Eskimo.' But he proved what an 'Eskimo' from Alaska could do. General Pershing decorated him for valor, and said, 'I wish I had a hundred Pullens in my Army!'"

There was no mistaking the pride in the elderly mother's voice as she told this story by the fireside that rainy evening in Skagway. Ma Pullen had lived the kind of adventure I hoped to find in Alaska.

Monday was coming. I had to make a decision. Should I return to Juneau on the boat? Or should I stay a bit longer and try to find work?

While I pondered this over coffee in Skagway's only restaurant, one of my boat friends came in and told me: "Say, I hear they're looking for a cook at one of the section houses on the railroad. You might try that."

So on Monday morning bright and early, I appeared at the railroad office and inquired about the job.

"I can't cook very well," I said, "But I can sure learn!"

Either he liked my style or he was desperate (I suspect the latter), because he hired me on the spot. I was to leave on the train the next day, heading for Glacier, a section house fourteen miles from Skagway on the White Pass Trail, to cook for a crew of four men and myself—and I couldn't boil water without scorching it!

# Chapter Five

## WAIT PATIENTLY AND YOU'LL RIDE

### September 1945

As I headed for the train the next morning, the wind was blowing viciously, as it can in Skagway. My hair was pulled this way and that. My hair kept getting into my eyes, but I couldn't push it back because my hands were busy—in one was the bundle of blankets the railroad guys had given me, and in the other was my own suitcase.

It paid to travel light in those days because you had to carry it all yourself. There were no porters and very few generous one-armed Good Samaritans around. Everyone else was busy carrying his own, too.

My bundle of blankets was what the old hobos used to call a "bindle" (bundle), and so the name: "bindle stiff." An uncle of mine who had bummed around a lot during the Great Depression told me about bindle stiffs. I have often reflected that this was a fitting beginning for my hobo life. A week in Alaska and I was already a "bindle stiff."

Steam from the engine swirled around my feet as I climbed aboard. The passenger car was right out of the Gay Nineties. I couldn't believe it. It probably dated back to the Gold Rush itself. It was actually lighted by gas lamps from the ceiling, and at the far end of the car, because it was getting to the chilly season, there was a tiny pot-bellied stove with a fire in it. The porter came along every so often and poked another stick of wood in the fire. I shook my head in wonder; had I stepped back fifty years in time? The train answered my thought with the traditional steam whistle's lonely wail that echoed in the canyons.

I had read a little about the White Pass & Yukon Railroad in the Seattle libraries, and I was glad I had. Just as there were not many towns in Alaska, libraries were very scarce as well. Most towns had just a small reading room with a modest collection of books, mostly fiction. A town of 300 souls, like Skagway, had few resources for anything more ambitious.

So here I was, riding into history, very much aware of it but only with the slightest notion of the sheer drama involved. I knew the railroad had been built during the gold rush, and that it was such a

*Tunnel across from Glacier Station at Mile 14 on the White Pass & Yukon Railroad.*

Lone E. Janson

difficult task that the initials "WP&Y" were commonly translated to "Wait Patiently & You'll Ride."

I knew there was a place out along the track where the railroad grade had been chiseled out of solid vertical rock with no foothold. Michael Heney, the builder himself, was the first over the edge of the cliff, with nothing to hold him but a rope from the top, making the first dynamite hole in the rock face.

After that, the "bully boys" of the railroad turned to the job with a will, and soon there was a ledge a little over three feet wide for the passage of the train.

Three feet wide is "narrow-gauge," a design that allows for tighter turns, and White Pass certainly needed tight turns in its myriad steep canyons. At the end of this famous cut they had to drill a tunnel.

I would be at the Glacier Section House a week before I found out that this famous cliff face and tunnel looked right opposite the section house where I worked. My window looked over that famous cut and tunnel! I was looking at that bit of history every day!

Aboard the train as the miles clipped off, the little train climbed ever higher into the dizzy, steep canyons. Far below I caught glimpses here and there of the original gold rush trail, a footpath hardly a foot wide, still beaten to bare earth after all these years.

Someone pointed out the site of White Pass City below. I tried to spot it, but all I could see was the smallest of clearings, hardly big enough for one cabin, let alone a "city." Alongside roared the plunging devil of a glacier-fed mountain torrent. How could there have been a "city" there beside the river, I wondered.

And still we climbed upward. Everything, I reflected, was on a Paul Bunyan scale except our little Tom Thumb railroad!

Only 22 miles from Skagway, which was at sea level, was the summit of White Pass (and the boarder with Canada) at 2,885 feet. The train had to climb more than a hundred vertical feet per mile, at the same time turning and twisting its way up the sides of the steep canyons. It was mind-boggling!

But I was only going to Mile 14, Glacier Station. At last the train huffed to a noisy, steam-hissing stop—more of a pause than a stop—because all they had to dump off was one teen-age cook for the section house at Glacier.

*Lone E. Janson*

*Inspiration Point on White Pass & Yukon Railroad, looking toward Glacier Station below.*

I hopped off with my small "bindle" and stood there watching the train, pulled by two engines, puffing and snorting up the steep grade across the canyon and then disappearing into the tunnel, waving a farewell handkerchief of smoke.

"Well," I thought, "If it's adventure I want, I certainly have it!" I looked around at a world so alien it could have been the moon. It was so high and steep it staggered the imagination!

All I could see was canyon—sheer rock canyon, rising straight up on one side and plunging straight down on the other side. Rock, scrubby trees, and the cold slice of the wind surrounded me.

The only thing horizontal in this vertical world was the railroad track, only a few feet wide, and the section house that was built out over the canyon, propped up by a forest of pilings.

The men were out to welcome me, and the welcome was genuine. If there is one certainty in this life beyond death and taxes, it is this: the cook is always welcome!

I was shown to a stark, bare room that was mine, all mine, such as it was. I stood in this grim, gray chamber surveying the bare metal cot, the cold light coming through the curtain-less window, and wondered, what next?

Here I was, fourteen miles from the nearest town, up in a canyon on the "Gold Rush trail," cooking for four men and myself, alone in the knowledge that I really didn't know anything about cooking.

The fellow who had been dubbing in as cook was an Indian named Ben. I liked him immediately as he showed me around the Spartan kitchen, and I watched everything he did with a desperate eye to remembering exactly, right down the last black cloud of pepper he put in the salad.

After showing me the big walk-in cooler and a few other details, he departed on the next train for a two-day binge that lasted two weeks. I was alone in my despair.

There was plenty to do as I turned to my new job. The crew boss was Bill Cook, and I found him friendly, helpful and full of tales of Gold Rush Skagway.

One of the crew was a tall, insolent fellow who took an immediate dislike to me and soon the feeling was mutual. Being young and inexperienced, I had not learned that in remote, claustrophobic situations like section houses, fishing boats, and the like, you need to do a lot of "going out of your way" to be pleasant even when you don't want to. Later I learned that a little restraint at the right time could make a big difference.

Almost as soon as Ben had left, I knew I was in trouble. Nevertheless, I plunged in trying to learn this job. Cooking was not really my "bag," but I really tried. My mother had weathered the Great Depression, and she taught me a lot about how to weather tough times. She had a few homilies that helped her out and now I resorted to them.

I found myself in an unknown world, almost like another planet. I had never encountered frozen cows or cold storage eggs, or some of the other weird things I encountered here.

The first time I went into the freezer unit, my jaw dropped. I had never seen frozen meat. At home, all meats in the stores were non-frozen, still bleeding, and labeled what kind of meat it was.

Now I was confronted with half a cow, frozen solid. I wondered how I was going to saw that solid-frozen cow—with a handsaw? I found out very quickly how tough it was to cut frozen meat by hand! That sucker was SOLID! Mostly I would saw off a chunk of something and put it in the stew pot.

The next problem was that I didn't have a recipe book. So I began to collect recipes from any likely or unlikely source. I found that can labels were a good source, but of course they only related to the contents of the can involved.

Later, I found a few large recipe books in the kitchen drawers, so I started looking through one. It turned out to be an advanced chef's cooking handbook. It was written in the most complicated language of the trade. I remember it recommended making copious quantities of white sauce for use in a wide variety of dishes.

"What the heck is white sauce?" I wondered. Luckily I declined to make the huge amount it recommended. If I had, I would have been drowning in white sauce, and I didn't even know what it was!

Occasionally I ran up against something I understood. Some apples were sent up the line, and I undertook to make an apple pie. I cut the apples and added the sugar and spices and then turned to the making of the crust.

I opened my cookbook. The recipe in the book said, "Take a

hundred-pound sack of flour, a five-pound can of lard..." I knew about how to cut a recipe, but how many cups of flour were there in a hundred-pound sack of flour?

I resorted to guesswork and to my amazement it came out okay. The crust was a bit tough, but the guys had good teeth and I chalked up the pie as a success.

When I told Bill Cook about the recipe I had found, he almost choked on his pie.

"You found those old Army recipes?" he laughed.

"Army recipes?" I asked. I knew that the Army had been in the Aleutians, but...?

"The 770th Railway Operating Battalion was in charge of the White Pass & Yukon Railroad during the building of the Alcan Highway," explained Bill. "It was the only central position on the route of the Alcan Highway that was accessible by any kind of transportation at all. Those fellows once took thirty-four trains over the summit in one day. They used to say White Pass was 'too cold for Polar Bears, and too steep for mountain goats.' There were even times that the wheels froze to the tracks." Bill paused to take another bite of pie, thinking about it. Then he shook his head and chuckled, "So you found those old Army recipes!"

Well, it HAD been an adventure, and now I knew why there were such strange recipes lying around in the kitchen drawers.

I felt good about the pie, so I tried a cake. I felt I knew, more or less, how to cut the hundred pound sack of flour. And I had found almost a full crate of eggs in a box.

I prepared the flour, baking powder, sugar and such, and got a couple of eggs from the crate. I cracked that first egg right into the prepared flour.

The egg was rotten! Not only rotten, but stinking rotten!

Gagging from the stench, I dumped the whole shebang into the canyon! I had to clean up the bowl and start over.

This time, I determined, I'd crack the eggs into a saucer first. The next egg in the separate saucer was rotten also! Over the rail into the canyon again. Rinse the saucer and try again. Same song, second verse. On and on, until many eggs later I had finally found one good egg. But I still needed another. I was so happy about the first one, I tried another in the same saucer, and lost the one good one I had attained the first time. Both went into the canyon with the others.

To bring the story to the end, I cracked over a half a case (not just a box, I mean a full CASE of boxes!) of those eggs—one at a time, throwing the rotten ones into the canyon, rinsing the dish, and trying again—before I had the two eggs I needed. By then all the doors and windows were open because of the stench of rotten eggs.

Incidentally, the cake turned out a resounding success, and in the process I had learned about "cold-storage eggs."

Over the years, cold-storage eggs were the norm in Alaska. Most Alaskans preferred cold-storage eggs; the Sourdoughs said fresh eggs had "no flavor"!

Nevertheless, I never ran into such rotten ones as I found at the Glacier Section House!

So I had learned about frozen cows, Army recipes, and cold-storage eggs. Now I was ready to approach milk. There were two types of milk: "armored cow," and "Klim."

I had always loved milk, and drank absolutely gallons of it at home. But now fresh milk was unheard of, and all that was available was evaporated or powdered milk. The powdered variety, called "Klim," was completely unpalatable and was only used in cooking, unless you had been in "the bush" for about fifty years and had no palate left. Klim is one reason, I suspect, that old sourdoughs tended to drink whiskey instead!

Klim (milk spelled backward) absolutely refused to mix with water. If you mixed some up, which everybody with kids tried to do, you usually drank the whitened water and chewed up the lumps. Kids were tough in early Alaska.

I wasn't that tough yet, so I worked on the "armored cow" (canned evaporated milk). I had a hard time learning to eat my cereal with canned milk, but learn I did, and since I really missed the tall cold glasses of fresh milk I had at home, I even learned to drink it by diluting it and adding a bit of honey. Every restaurant in Alaska in those days had cans of evaporated milk on the counters for use in coffee; the most elegant restaurants put it in little pitchers, but it was still "armored cow"! Most Alaskans learned to prefer it. In Seattle you could always tell an Alaskan: he was the guy who asked for canned milk for his coffee instead of fresh cream, and complained that fresh eggs had "no flavor."

I thought I was making progress, but that was fiction. I liked working at the section house, and I loved that raw, deep canyon.

But between cold storage eggs, Klim, armored cow, and the walk-in freezer, I knew I was in over my head. And those were minor compared to the weekly grocery requisitions.

Every Friday I had to make out a list of groceries I would need. I put it in an envelope, tied a piece of string around it and put it on a forked stick, to be picked up with the mail by the next passing train.

For the first couple of weeks I ordered almost nothing, not knowing what to order or how to cook it when I got it. By the third week, all sorts of supplies were running low, and my confidence was beginning to take effect (prematurely, of course, but one must start somewhere), so I sat down and made out a requisition to end all requisitions.

I ordered cases of this and that, things that I could cook from the labels I had read, and the order was long. Judgment is another thing you don't learn overnight, especially as a teenager. But again, one must start somewhere. They must have gone into orbit at headquarters when they got that supply requisition; it was enough to feed the 770th Railway Battalion for a year!

By now I was writing excited letters home all about everything, including describing how to mail a letter! To mail a letter, I had to put it in an envelope, tie a piece of string around it and put it on a forked stick. When I heard the train whistle I'd go out, hold the stick out close to the tracks, and the conductor would scoop the letter off on the fly as he went past.

If I didn't have a stamp (which I usually didn't), I'd just tape the three pennies to the envelope. Mail to be received was simply tossed out as the train headed for the summit. A flag alongside the track signaled the train if you wanted to go to town to shop or for a dance, and the train would stop or sort of slow down so you could hop aboard.

The section house was also served by telephone, a single line for the whole 110 miles from Skagway to Whitehorse. It was one of those old-fashioned crank jobbies, and each section house had its own code ring. Glacier was three long and two short rings. And of course, everyone could listen in. It was almost expected.

Our section house perched out over a deep, steep canyon. The view from the "back porch" was almost straight down. I couldn't guess how far you'd fall if there was an accident. Despite the steepness and depth of the canyon, the bears found it easy to climb up there and help themselves (mostly at night) and raid the garbage can. That was all right, but one of the bears had a playful habit of kicking the can down into the canyon when he got his fill. That was one steep canyon down there, and the men were getting a little annoyed at having to climb down there and haul the can back up.

One day one of the guys alerted me, hissing: "Look!" Our little black bear was enjoying smorgasbord in the garbage can. As soon as he was aware of us he left.

"He isn't going to kick the can down into the canyon tonight," the boss told me. "We went out there today and wired that can firmly to the back platform! We used really stout wire for it, too!"

That night there was a terrific commotion in the darkness outside. The bear had apparently eaten what he wanted from the can, but when he tried to give it his customary kick, the can refused to move!

Now, bears have what might be termed a "whim of iron," so Bruin started kicking and banging that can and making an unholy racket. He did plenty of damage to it, but the boys had done a good job of wiring, so Bruin at last turned to some other object on which to vent his wrath. He found the tin washtub hanging on the back balcony, and the next morning we found that tub halfway across the canyon! And he looked like such a small bear!

Of course, everyone connected with the railroad learned about our regular backyard visitor. One day an engineer on the railroad came up to see us, saying he wanted a bear rug. We had a good visit and a meal, such as it was. Then the engineer laid his trap. He put some meat on the back platform for the bear and took up a waiting vantage point with a flashlight and his gun handy, while the rest of us turned in to sleep.

Toward morning a shot rang out, and we all got up to find what had happened. The engineer was excited, of course, and proceeded to tell what he had done in that dark night.

"I got that bear right between the eyes," he asserted. "I flashed the light out there and his big green eyes lit up like Christmas. When

I shot him, he made a funny kind of hissing noise, and I heard him crashing in the brush. Just in case, we better not go out to find him until daylight." The account was accompanied by coffee and other bear stories around the table till morning began to tinge the sky, and finally enough daylight crept down the canyon walls to afford light for the bear search.

They never found a bear; what they found was Bill Cook's cat—shot between the eyes. The poor engineer had a hard time living that down, even though a later trip bagged the bear.

That bear had been just a small blackie, but he could have been a serious danger. Small it might have been, but when they dragged the carcass back up the trail, I saw just how big even a small bear could be. He probably weighed about 500 pounds. I wondered if that fellow ever told anyone the whole story of how he got his bear rug.

As much as I was enjoying the surroundings, my inexperience as a cook was bound to have become an issue sooner or later.

One day the boys decided to take me on a trip up the line on the "speeder." The speeder must have had a small engine on it because we didn't pump it. Also it was fully open to the air and the cold wind. But oh, what a beautiful trip through the canyons of White Pass! I didn't realize it at the time because the guys were being so nice, but this wasn't a sightseeing trip.

As we sped along, there were canyons all around and side canyons beyond them. I had never seen so much rock so steeply upended in my life. White Pass has a way of being warm and sheltered in one side canyon, while the main canyon may be filled with billowing white fog, driven by a wind capable of cutting like a frozen hacksaw. As we started out, headed for the tunnel across the canyon, I could see the fog cottoning its way down the next canyon. On we went, through the tunnel, around a bend or two, and then we were in the midst of the fog. Everything was white and I was totally without any bearings except for the railroad tracks themselves leading the way into white nothing. I loved the fog; it gave the wild surroundings a mysterious quality.

We slippered our way through the fog, every sound cushioned and deadened, every impression cut off at the limit of the fog. It was cold and there was also wind, which made it worse. Shivering, I huddled down into my coat. In those days I had not heard of "Chill Factor." I shuddered, but I was not sure if I was cold or excited.

*Lone E. Janson*

*The Canteliver Bridge on the White Pass & Yukon Railroad.*

That's when we came to the High Bridge. My first impression of this breathtaking bridge with its angular steel supports was the sight of a bridge ending in white fog with no bottom to the canyon or end to the bridge. It was like stepping into a fiction story, only this was real!

Of course, that wasn't the message the boys wanted conveyed. They were taking me to a section house up the line where they pointed out, "They serve THREE kinds of meat for dinner!" Indeed they did. I believe it was chicken, ham and beef. It was a good dinner, an excellent dinner, and I enjoyed the outing immensely. But I really felt inadequate after that meal. I knew I could never cook like that.

Meanwhile, those fellows up there treated me with utmost respect, and even with a little grudging affection. Looking back, I have to acknowledge all the things they did to make my stay more pleasant. They offered very cautious hints on cooking techniques, calculated not to injure the teenage feminine cook sensitivity (heavy on the "cook" part, because the "Code-of-the-North-about-the-Care-and-Treatment-of-Cooks" was in operation here).

If I hadn't been so totally inexperienced, so thoroughly out of place in a kitchen in general, I might have stayed for quite a while at Glacier, and it would have been a good life, too.

The trouble was that I wanted adventure that was not of the culinary sort. I appreciate the things they did, and the ways in which they did it. For my money, the old-time Alaskan is the smoothest male article going. They were rough looking, tough talking, and hard working, but could also be sensitive and sweet.

September was almost over and winter was in the air. The mountains were glorious with fall, and blueberry pies were in the oven.

Then one day the snow appeared on the mountains above us. After that, each day found it a little farther down, until it reached our own canyon. The first snow of the season is often breathtakingly beautiful. I ran out onto the balcony (where the bear-baiting garbage cans were) with a skillet in my hand to watch the huge, fluffy flakes swirling in the air over the wild canyon.

One Sunday afternoon I was sitting in the dining room trying to beat a game of solitaire. Time had sneaked up on me and I didn't realize it was so late—almost time for dinner. I looked up and there was the tall, insolent guy standing above me.

"I'm hungry," he growled. "When are we going to have dinner?"

His tone rubbed me the wrong way and I snapped, "When I get ready to cook it." I had not yet learned that special isolated-situation restraint mentioned before.

Later he growled, "You don't know how close you came to getting fired."

What made the whole thing worse is that I knew I was in the wrong. That really got under my skin. I knew then that I might as well take whatever money I had earned and move on. I wasn't "making the cut" as a cook.

I knew that in Fairbanks I could make pretty good money as a waitress, and there were lots of other places I wanted to see. It was time to make another try.

I was getting ready to give my notice, but they were faster than I was. The letter was in the bundle they tossed off the speeding train. I had to marvel at its tact: "And although we know that you have tried..." (I grinned because it was a masterpiece of understatement and tact) "We find that due to your inexperience..."

My first job in Alaska, and I was fired. My reaction was a mixture of pain and relief. No more Friday grocery requisitions, no more Army recipes and lumpy gravy. I was going to see people again—lots of them,

*Lone E. Janson*

whole towns full! It had been a pretty lonesome hitch for an eighteen-year-old girl, and I was ready to move on.

# Chapter Six

## BOREDOM AND DEMOGRAPHICS
### Whitehorse—October 1945

Once more I hopped on the train with my little "bindle" and headed back down the trail to Skagway to pick up my paycheck. When the bookkeeper found out that I was headed to the interior, he gave me a free pass on the railroad as far as Whitehorse.

There was no reason to linger in Skagway and adventure called.

Again the little steam engine puffed its way up toward the summit of White Pass and parts unknown beyond. A month in White Pass was not long enough to rob it of its splendor. White Pass City still caused me to shake my head. There was hardly room for one tent, let alone a tent city. Inspiration Point was still incredible with its tiny foot trail, huge canyons and icy winds.

I felt a special twinge passing Glacier Station, then the difficult cliff-cut across the canyon and the tunnel. Once more I crossed the High Bridge, but this time I could see the other side and the train gave me a sense of security that had been elusive the first time.

Then I was in new territory. In only a few more miles we were at the summit and Lake Bennett, where hordes of 1898 Klondike stampeders had built their boats for the trip down the Yukon, to Dawson in Canada.

We stopped at Bennett for lunch. I looked at the fine family-style food with new appreciation. I had at least a smidgen of experience to call on now. I was learning what made a good camp-style meal.

From Bennett we came into a new kind of country, one that I suppose you could call the High Plateau. From the summit of the mountains there seemed no descent. Now the country took on a new aspect: one of wide-open spaces. Sparse little trees, skinny as pencils, now replaced the huge lush ones of the Southeast rain forest.

One thing I was learning about Alaska was the absolute drenching of the senses: the great wide vistas or the steep, dizzy ones; the fragile loveliness, followed by scenes of almost savage beauty. Then they were followed by "miles and miles of miles and miles." Everything on such a grand scale; everything had a feeling of wilderness, survival, and history.

Robert Service called it "The freshness, the freedom, the farness..." and that was a very good description.

Finally we arrived in Whitehorse. My grand adventure was getting well under way again at last.

After the cramped streets and spaces of Southeast Alaska, squeezed in by abrupt mountains and fiords, Whitehorse seemed such a roomy town. It sat on a wide, flat area along the banks of the Yukon River. It was still full of Army personnel, both U.S. and Canadian.

I had to wait a couple of days to take my bus to Fairbanks, so I settled into my hotel room. I was too young to go in the bars where all the action was, so I spent a lonely time of it. In those days, bars were not necessarily places to drink so much as places to socialize, meet friends and talk.

It was small wonder that young people felt lost, bored, and left out. Even the movie theaters usually only ran once of twice a week.

I spent hours in the hotel working crossword puzzles when I could find them and reading boring stories. None of them were about Alaska, and Alaska was what I wanted to read about.

Mostly I just wandered the streets. I had no pleasant pal like Ted to keep me company, but I did what I could to fend off loneliness. Loneliness, I had already learned, was merely a temporary state, easily erased by activity and work.

Actually, Whitehorse was the scene of my "Adventure that Never Happened." That adventure was the riverboat to Dawson.

I had to make a decision about my next move, and I was told that the last sternwheeler of the season was preparing to leave the next day for Dawson. There was that air of excitement in Whitehorse that I had encountered in Southeast Alaska when a boat was due. Oh, how I wanted to go on it! To Dawson and the Klondike country! It would be like reliving history.

I wandered down to the riverfront to look wistfully at the wooden river queens, one ready to sail, the other ready to go into winter quarters. It was probably the "Keno" getting ready to sail that day in October 1945.

At that time, the sternwheelers still burned wood. They had to stop along the river every eight hours to load up on wood for the boilers, and Native people along the river supplemented their subsistence living by supplying that wood. I had never been on a sternwheeler, and longed to find out what it felt like to move along a river by paddlewheel.

How was I to know it would all be gone and changed in such a very short time? Within a few years the sternwheelers converted to oil, and then with the advent of aviation, they ceased running altogether.

As I stood on the bank of the Yukon River I didn't know how close the future was, but I knew I ached with the knowledge of what I was missing. It was the kind of adventure I had come north to experience.

I fingered my WP&Y paycheck and considered very carefully. I knew for an absolute, irrevocable fact that if I went to Dawson I was there for the winter. There would likely be no work available during the winter. No planes, no boats, probably not ever a dog sled would be available to get out. Given my tiny horde of money—that one paycheck, period—I thought long and hard.

Whitehorse. River paddleboats. Yukon River to Dawson. Wood refueling stops. What a thing I missed!

Considering the history involved, I should have done it. But then, I was very young and a little scared (certainly awestruck by the country) and there was one more very practical reason. Dawson was in Canada and I simply didn't know if I needed a passport or something, or if there were special restrictions for U.S. persons in Canada who wanted to stay and work. I wasn't sure of the questions to ask or where to ask them in order to find out. So with one more wistful look at the lovely riverboats, I wandered back to my hotel.

But I knew that in Alaska adventure was everywhere. I was young and eager, so I considered the alternatives. In my mind, Whitehorse had been a way-stop en route to Dawson, but now I knew that because of the Alcan Highway opening, Whitehorse had suddenly and very recently become a way-stop on the way to Fairbanks, Alaska.

O'Harra Bus Lines had sent their very first bus over the new highway the week before, and the next one would leave in two or three days. That was a good alternative. Fairbanks was back in U.S. territory, probably not so isolated and with better chances for a job. There was the adventure of traveling on a bus line over a brand new and very historic highway on the second civilian bus ever. Only one before mine!

*Lone E. Janson*

I had always been into the history of events like this. I went over in my mind what I knew of the building of that highway. It wasn't just the actual construction that made the story. There had been a long and frustrating campaign by the people of the Territory of Alaska all during the '20s and '30s for a land link to the "Old Country" (which we called the "South 48" then). There had been several steamship strikes that had plunged Alaskans into near starvation, but government policy was still to ignore Alaska. A highway remained a pipe dream.

One of the arguments that had been the hardest to overcome had been the impossibility of building through Canada's tundra-mountain terrain. Tragic tales were cited of the suffering and death of thousands during the Gold Rush who had tried to cross overland through Canada to the Klondike.

To counter this, many publicity efforts had been made to dramatize that the route was feasible. One of the most dramatic had been a 3,000-mile dog sled trip by "Slim" Williams.

Slim was a sourdough who had crossed Valdez Glacier in 1898 and had stayed on to become one of Alaska's most famous dog mushers and to pioneer cross-breeding Huskies with wolves.

The team he took to the "Outside" in the '30s was part wolf. The purpose of the trip, sponsored and encouraged by Alaska Delegate "Tony" Dimond, was to prove the feasibility of the overland route.

Feasible it might have been, and the crowds loved the parade in Washington, D.C., when Slim drove his dog sled, mounted on wheels, down the Capital's streets. But the political reaction in the South 48 was still one of general malaise, as with most things Alaskan.

With the onset of World War II, Alaskans thought the highway was a certainty, but Canada resisted. A highway leads both ways and the threat of invasion via Alaska was a real concern. Under the circumstances, one cannot blame Canada for being rather unenthused about a highway just then.

But the Russians were fighting too, and they needed thousands of airplanes that had to be sent to that beleaguered country. DC-3s didn't have the range of flight that we have now, to get across Canada and Alaska to Nome.

The solution was a series of airfields for the DC-3s to get from Great Falls, Montana, via a route through Canada, to Fairbanks or

Nome, Alaska, where Russian pilots took over and flew them across the Bering Sea.

Those airports needed support, and that included the ones in Canada. Hence Canada joined the effort, and the Alcan Highway was undertaken to advance the War Effort.

The only mid-way access was the White Pass & Yukon Railroad, so that's why those Army recipes had been at the Glacier Section House.

The effort to build the highway took less than a year. On September 25, 1942, the two main crews from the south and from the north met at Contact Creek, Mile 590. The highway, rough and rugged, was done.

In the three years since its completion, there had been little time to improve it. When I arrived in Whitehorse in the first week of October 1945, it was still a military road, closed to civilian traffic unless specifically approved. Every rut and pothole was G.I., and I think the new civilian buses saluted them all.

Once my mind was made up to go, I eagerly purchased my ticket at the hotel desk.

With a couple of days to wait, I sat in the lobby reading everything I could find: newspapers, magazines, whatever.

In this random reading I came across some population figures that intrigued me. I read that the population of Alaska was less than 100,000 at that time, 90,000 and some. Heaven knows I had time on my hands, so I began to do some figuring, just to relieve the boredom.

The Territory of Alaska had an area of 586,000 square miles, so I figured the population density was about one person per SIX SQUARE MILES! Of the cities I had seen, only Ketchikan and Juneau were likely to have a population of over a thousand. Others that big might have been Fairbanks and possibly Anchorage, because of the war. (The military was hard to calculate because it was so fluid, and of course there had been no census since the war began.) My limited experiences with Alaska made the "one person per six square miles" seem about right.

With nothing else to do, I carried this equation a bit further. There must have been at least ten men to every woman, although I think the male ratio was even higher. That would spread the female population to about one woman per SIXTY square miles, and most of them were married. I tried to visualize a sixty-mile square of wilderness with myself the only woman in it—and I was single!

# Chapter Seven

## ALCAN HIGHWAY

### Early October 1945

Morning found me sitting in the lobby sipping coffee and yawning, waiting for the bus to take me to my own "sixty-mile square" of Alaska.

When the bus came up next to the hotel, I found that it was much like an old yellow school bus. You know the kind: innocent of extra springs and seat upholstery and such frills. Still, all in all, it was more than acceptable in a true frontier land. We were following a pioneer highway, after all. Why be spared the full effect of those bottomless potholes and muddy ruts?

I joined a few others climbing aboard, and we drove around White horse picking up people waiting in other parts of town. Among those picked up was another young woman, but there were no seats close to me so we didn't meet right away.

Because we were crossing back into U.S. territory again, the bus wound up back at the hotel lobby, where we went through military clearance. First, the U.S. Army MPs boarded and checked us all out. Then the Royal Canadian Mounted Police, complete with red coats, did their checkout.

My I.D. at that time was the Coast Guard clearance card that I had obtained to work aboard the "baby flattop" Liscomb Bay on its trial during World War II. My clearance card read bluntly: "Lone Green: MESS"! The wordage seemed hilarious to us civilians, but neither Canadian nor U.S. military cracked a smile!

As a sideline, the Liscomb Bay was torpedoed and sunk during the war, and it was recorded that the torpedo had hit the ship in the "mess hall." They said there was cabbage and food all over when the ship went down.

Later, I assumed (incorrectly) that the Liscomb Bay had been named in honor of the Fort Liscum in Valdez during the gold rush. I thought it an honorable name.

At last we set out along the dusty, chuckhole-pitted trail that was the newborn Alcan Highway. We bounced along for miles without seeing much more than porcupines scurrying for cover, squirrels darting across the road, and a few rabbits. Scrubby spruce trees, tall and skinny, looking more like pipe cleaners than trees, grew from the impoverished-looking soil. We called them "pencil trees," and in later years I learned they were characteristic of what the Russians called "taiga," which is the name for this type of ecosystem. It is far from impoverished, but that's the impression it conveys.

The driver pulled over briefly to let us view the historic old trading post of Champagne. Its collection of log buildings was arranged around an open space. It was very historic and dated back to the days of '98 when cattle were driven to Dawson along the Dalton Trail.

The driver explained how this colorful old post got its name. After Jack Dalton had successfully driven the first herd of cattle into the Yukon, he uncorked a case of champagne at the grand opening. A great time was had by one and all, and it was promptly dubbed "Champagne, Yukon Territory."

Some of the passengers on the bus ventured to suggest that our own trip was on a historical par with that occasion, so where was the champagne? We all laughed as the bus started up again in a cloud of October dust. It had not yet snowed, so the roads were dry and dusty.

The rattling and creaking of the bus over the rough road made conversation difficult. The few exchanges between myself and fellow passengers forced us to shout over the din, so we abandoned the effort after a while, although there was plenty to comment on. We lapsed into silence, each of us wrapped in our noise-enforced isolation, watching the miles unfold.

Enveloped in this cocoon of noise-silence, I descended into a long, weary reverie about my Alaskan venture so far.

The voyage north had been wonderful, and I had racked up an amazing amount of adventure in a single month in Alaska. But there was something missing. It occurred to me that those lopsided ratios of men to women that I had toyed with in the Whitehorse Hotel had a meaning that I had missed. It didn't mean so much that a woman had a good chance of finding a man as it meant that she was likely to be very lonely for a "best friend" of her own age and sex, whether she was married or not. It was an interesting insight into what demographics really mean.

The bus hit a particularly deep bump that lifted me off the seat and put me down again hard. I came out of this reverie to join the rest of the crew in a collective exchange of half-shouted comments that could not be heard over the noise of the bus. But the moment had joined us together in lip reading and body language for a while, and we were companions again.

The beauty of the country now registered again on my consciousness. It was a country of long, skinny lakes, gloriously lovely as Canadian scenery is. I watched mile after bumpy mile unfold with scarcely another thought of myself.

The condition of the road kept our speed to about 25 miles per hour, making it a slow, tedious drive, and finally night fell.

The road followed the large and historic Kluane Lake for a number of miles till we came to the head of it and the old fur-trading town of Burwash Landing.

At last the bus slowed down and made a sharp turn onto a steep, rutted drive down to Burwash Landing Lodge on Kluane Lake.

Here our bedraggled crew of travelers was able to wash up and gather in the big, comfortable lobby to await dinner. It was nice to talk and be heard again, and we had a grand time visiting.

To my dismay, one of the passengers dominated the conversation, insisting that Canada should be a part of the United States. He developed this theme at length, despite the obvious discomfiture of our Canadian hosts and the sour looks from Americans who could see its inappropriateness. Fortunately his discourse was cut short by the call to dinner.

A funny thing happened at Burwash Landing—the cows came home. As we dined on a sumptuous meal of Dall mountain sheep swimming in rich brown gravy and vegetables fresh from the garden, the owner told us: "The cows always come home just before the first snowfall." It seems they had a herd of cows that more or less wandered about during the summer, but their annual return to the warmth of the barn always heralded snow.

The evening passed pleasantly in the lobby with a wide range of conversation. In those days of little radio (some short-wave was picked up), no television, and few other forms of diversion, conversation was a fine art.

Stories of incidents and adventures of the local trappers and sub-sistence hunters were told over and over, until they were polished into "literary gems." The conversation was thus amusing and intelligent, informative and entertaining.

I was beginning to learn that a fine storyteller was highly respected in early Alaska and Canada.

Engrossed in the stories, I didn't have a chance to become acquaint-ed with the other woman on the bus until we went to the room we were assigned to share.

Her name was Nelda O'Laughlin, and she was a nurse. Like myself, she was single and had come to Alaska looking for work, and I suspect, a tad of adventure too.

Since there was no electricity, we were given a Blazo mantle lamp to light when we wished. I had never seen one before. I was thoroughly familiar with the old kerosene wick lamp, having grown up with them, but this Blazo mantle lamp was a new one on me.

Fortunately Nelda, my roomie, knew how to light it. She pumped it up, lit it, fiddled with knobs and made mysterious incantations over it. It finally settled into a brilliant white light. Both the hissing noise and its brightness amazed me. It sure beat the old kerosene lamp, and one could read by its light in great comfort.

And so we visited, read, and slept in this famous old hostelry that first night on the Alcan Highway.

The next day before starting out again, we had a hearty breakfast of sourdough hotcakes and all the trimmings. Sure enough, there were dark snow clouds in the sky and that sense of impending storm.

The hostess handed the driver a huge brown-bag lunch and a large thermos of coffee. There were no restaurants or roadhouses on that fledgling Alcan Highway.

The road passed through country alternately barren in its taiga-appearance, and then spectacular in the splendor of lakes and mountains. Gradually the clouds descended lower and lower, and at last, just as predicted by the cows, it began to snow. There was a mystical beauty to the flakes swirling down gently around us.

Suddenly a moose appeared on the road ahead. The bus stopped, the moose stopped, and we regarded each other. The moose must have felt we were sorry specimens indeed, because he shook his big antler as if in disgust, then stepped off the road with great dignity and was lost in the swirling snow.

That little burst of excitement settled down again into the boredom of miles of high-decibel, slow travel on a bumpy road. Time passed. I was beginning to get hungry. We stopped at the Alaska-Canada border. The snow had paused, and the driver parked the bus in a spectacular spot. All around was sheer wilderness, marked only by a deep cut in the brush about five feet wide and straight as a plumb line from one horizon to the other.

I learned later it was cut clear from the Arctic Ocean to Mt. St. Elias on the south, at exactly 141d. W. Longitude. This was the boarder between Canada and Alaska!

We parked where we could look clear to the horizon in both directions and ate our lunch. We had little dried-up apples, mountain sheep sandwiches, and lukewarm sweetened coffee. Some meals stand out in the memory, and this was one. Except for the sandwiches, its quality was nothing to rave about, but no restaurant I know could rival its spectacular location. We were back in Alaska again.

Our bus driver had a puckish sense of humor. He told us the tale of the fellow who had a trapping camp, or a spread of some kind, located right in the vicinity of the border. This was back in the Gold Rush Days when no one who lived there was sure just exactly where the border was. When the survey crews came through and finished measuring, they informed the old trapper that his location was on the Alaskan side of the border.

The old Sourdough breathed a sigh of relief, and said: "Oh, thank God! No more of those cold Yukon winters!"

We started up again, and the long tedious miles continued to unwind. The sky cleared as darkness descended. The stars began to wink out as I wearily watched. We were on the last lap of a long, rough, two-day trip and there was no question about it, I was tired. I laid my head back, looking at the stars in the clear night sky, along with an occasional high, thin cloud.

Suddenly it dawned on me that something unusual was going on. The stars were shining through that high thin cloud up there. I wondered how that could be? Most clouds, even high thin ones, will obscure starlight. That was sure a funny-looking cloud, I thought, peering intently at it.

*Lone E. Janson*

Someone said, "The Northern Lights are starting up!"

The first faint brilliance of the aurora was what I had seen in the sky. It was simply an early-season beginning for the wonders it would perform later in the Fairbanks winter. From wisps of gauze-like light, a waving curtain followed, then little flashes and swishes, glowing and fading and glowing again. It stayed with us all the way into Fairbanks until streetlight faded its glory and welcomed us into civilization again.

We made our way along the dark banks of the Chena River to our hotel in downtown Fairbanks. Nelda and I got off the bus, stiff-legged and yawning, and went into the coffee shop for a late sandwich before turning in. We were dusty and tired after the long journey; tomorrow would be soon enough to see what Fairbanks had in store for us. My first winter in Alaska!

We finished eating and went upstairs to bed. We had just settled down comfortably for our night's rest when both of us were jolted awake. We sat up and looked at each other.

"What the heck is that?" we both asked in the same breath.

From below our window came the alcoholically off-key and very loud restrains of: "Sweet Adoline..." in a drunken basso-alto voice. The unknown drunk kept it up most of the night, with only a few variations of song title and key, though it never improved in quality.

# Chapter Eight

## PEARL DIVING & FOOT IN MOUTH
### Fairbanks—October 1945

The next morning, Nelda and I were a bit travel-weary and bleary-eyed after the drunken serenade under our window the night before. After breakfast in the Nordale coffee shop, we fared out to look for work.

As a nurse, Nelda landed a job within a week—in Valdez. It was pronounced "Val-deez." That mystified me.

She had told me: "Valdez got its Spanish name from the famous Spanish admiral Valdes, but because the Spanish-American War was on at the time, the townsfolk didn't want the name to sound too Spanish! So they adopted the 'Val-DEEZ' pronunciation."

Nelda and I had a farewell dinner the night before she left. She was buying since she was the one who had a job. We were in a good mood, so everything was funny to us that evening.

Nearby, a big husky fellow ordered a New York cut steak, and admonished the waitress rather loudly in a kidding way: "Make sure it's a New York cut. I used to be a butcher and that's what I want!"

Nelda and I found this hilarious, and being in that goofy mood, I demanded, "How can you tell?"

He turned around and looked at me. My first impression was his eyes. They were sort of hazel-green, and they were laughing right along with us.

"You can't change the bone structure of a bovine," he replied.

I was taking in the effect of those merry green-hazel eyes with an electric pleasure.

Nelda fielded the perfect comeback: "I don't know about that. Since rationing in the war, I've seen a lot of things happen to the bone structure of a bovine!" We were off into peals of gaiety again.

Our funny bones were overactive that night. My friend Nelda was leaving and it was our last chance to enjoy each other's company. And there were those hazel eyes, and the rest of him wasn't bad either.

Nelda and I took in a movie, and then we went out dancing at a local bar before going home. I remember a vocalist singing: "Who's that coming through the door? A big fat butterfly!"

It was easy to get dances, and I had a wonderful time, even though it seemed strange to be dancing in boots. But then, everybody around was wearing boots too.

That night it was the howling of Huskies that kept us awake. I found the sound sad and haunting. It was a truly Alaskan sound, and I didn't really mind the fact that they were keeping me awake. The howling of Huskies was, well, Alaskan!

Nelda left the next morning. I was lonesome after she left, especially while I was looking for a job. I would walk around and stop into any little cafe I saw and ask for waitress work.

It was winter so waitress work was scarce. Over the next week or so I got a few odd jobs doing anything that came up.

One of the first was in a hotel for a week while their regular laundress was away on a trip. I only had to wash sheets and towels, but they had one of those brand new Bendix automatic washing machines with the little window in the front. I had never seen one before, but after someone showed me how the controls worked I rather enjoyed watching the sheets and towels wash automatically. The hotel also had a mangle, so I learned a different kind of ironing as well. It was all so new and different that it really impressed me.

Another time a small cafe needed a dishwasher just that very evening because their regular man was sick. I grabbed an apron and went to work right then and there "pearl diving" for a couple of nights.

In those days there were no modern dishwashers in cafes. There were only two huge sinks, three or four feet deep. One sink was filled to the brim with hot soapy water, the other with hot rinse water.

I was so short I had to stand on a wooden stool to reach into the water. When I bent over up to my armpits, sometimes I had my chin right into the suds.

I filled those first lonesome weeks with a lot of walking about, just looking. I learned that Fourth Avenue was the "Red Light" district. I learned that the bridge across Chena Slough led to Garden Island.

In summer there was only that bridge to Garden Island, but as temperatures plunged, Fairbanks gained a new street, paved with ice, right down the middle of Chena Slough, with traffic signs and marked intersections. A road that vanished with the arrival of breakup.

My favorite place for meeting people was a little cafe called the Hi-Spot. It was small but warm. It had only a tiny horseshoe counter with a friendly waitresses. It was always crowded with locals in from the cold looking for company and chitchat over coffee. I'd go there and enjoy fragrant hot coffee while my glasses thawed.

It was in this little cafe that I met an old sourdough, Fritz Larson, who took a fatherly interest in me. After one look at my flimsy "Outside" ("South 48") coat, he took me firmly in hand to the nearest clothing store. My protests were brushed aside like so many pesky mosquitoes.

He declared, "This is Fairbanks in the winter! You CAN'T go around like that!" Objections meant nothing. He made sure I had a long, well-lined coat, mukluks, mittens, and a woolen scarf long enough to encompass my neck, head, and across my nose and mouth.

"Now you wear those! And when the temperature drops to twenty below or colder, you pull that scarf across your face and whatever you do, DON'T BREATHE THROUGH YOUR MOUTH! You could frost a lung! Breathe through your nose!"

That was my introduction to the realities of an Arctic winter. Frost a lung? That didn't sound good at all, so I was very religious about breathing through my nose. I vividly recall the frost from my breath that gathered inside the woolen scarf as I walked through the beautiful Arctic night.

Fritz took me to my first real dance (not counting the farewell evening with Nelda when we danced in the cocktail lounge). He was a member of the band. It was the Tanana Valley Farmers Association Ball. Fritz lined up a whole range of partners for me to dance with, so I never sat one out!

I had a whale of a good time that evening. I also learned to do the Schottische, a lively dance indeed. Schottisches and polkas were THE dances of early Alaska.

I arrived in Fairbanks in mid-October, and my resources became tighter and tighter as Halloween came and went, and still no full-time job opened up for me. I never really went hungry, at least not very hungry, but I remember calculating the price of a sandwich (about a dollar) against the price of a full meal ($1.50 or so).

I figured that I got a lot for a full meal, so if I wasn't hungry enough to polish off the full meal, I wouldn't eat a sandwich. I was counting pennies, no doubt about it! I got down to about one square meal a day.

But if jobs were hard to come by, boyfriends were not. I was to find that just as Nature abhors a vacuum and tries to fill it, so Alaska abhorred a single woman. The women tried to match me up with eligible men, and eligible men fairly danced all sorts of favors upon me.

It was truly different from the "South 48"! But no one seemed to understand that I wanted to see Alaska, to enjoy being young and single, and try to see this great land—all of it, or at least as much as possible.

What no one seemed to realize was that I really wasn't interested in a romance. To me marriage would mean the end of my great adventure before I had a chance to really pursue it. It was obvious to me that I'd have no trouble finding a marriage partner when I was ready. The problem was how to stay single till I was ready.

First there was Pete. We got along well as just friends, and we went dancing a couple of times. He invited me to his home for Thanksgiving and I really enjoyed the hospitality. But every time I visited his family, I got the feeling that there was something sort of predatory going on. I began to avoid Pete, and the relationship died a natural death.

I went out a few times with another young fellow who spoke with an affected Southern accent. He wanted to get me in bed, which annoyed me tremendously. I tried to discourage him, but he wasn't getting the message, so I decided to be really cruel. One night I read poetry to him for a couple of hours! He never bothered me again.

As the thermometer continued its inexorable dive, I couldn't wear my glasses outside as they threatened to freeze to my face, so I carried them in my mittened hand inside my pocket while I scrunched over the snow in my mukluks. The minute I walked into the Hi Spot Café and pulled them out, in a flash the hot, steamy air caked them in ice (not frost—ICE) with miniature fern designs and all. There was nothing I could do except wait for them to thaw. My memories of that winter in Fairbanks tend to be rather blurry!

Those long walks through the Arctic night were my main pastime. The most bizarre memory I have is meeting a "flasher" on the street at 40 below zero. I had never encountered one before, and the only reaction I had was: "He'd better get that thing inside or he'll frost something besides a lung!" I chuckled all the way home, wishing Nelda was there so we could share the joke.

Soon after Thanksgiving I landed a waitress job at the old Pioneer Cafe. I reinstated my union card and went to work.

It was a nice coffee shop, and the clientele was pleasant. Located right down by Chena Slough, it was near the old bridge to Garden Island. I liked working there and having a job made it a little less lonesome. I'd finish my side work after midnight, close up, and walk home, enjoying the Arctic night.

Oh, the breathtaking grandeur of those walks! Snow on the ground had frozen and re-crystallized till it formed individual crystals sometimes half an inch across, crystals that mirrored the brilliance of the moonlight. They reminded me of those glittery Christmas cards I loved, only much brighter.

Overhead the clear northern sky was filled with millions of stars. They were not bright like those in the tropics, but tiny pinpoints of clear white, like strobe lights from far, far away. The moon was not that warm golden hue you see in warmer climes, but it was a clear sharp silver-white, so bright that the night was almost like daylight.

Exactly overhead was the North Star. Yes, right above us, in the center of the sky! This was the adventure I truly sought! Imagine being directly UNDER the North Star!

Sounds carried farther too, and the sound of a church bell across a frozen tundra field was enough to bring tears to the eyes, except that my eyes were already watering with the intense cold!

Those were the nights with no aurora. When the Northern Lights started their dance, it was just too beautiful for any words at all. I risked frostbite, frosted lungs, and frozen fingers and toes just to gaze in awe at the shifting patterns of light and color. Usually they were translucent green fading to blues and whites, and on occasion shifting to lavender and violet shades, and one time they turned red. They danced across the sky in varied patterns like rays and mists. But the most common was in the form of a waving gauze of light.

One thing about Northern lights, it's always dark and cold when they dance, so I could never stay for the whole show. I could only wear my glasses a short time in those severe temperatures. Then my glasses frosted over!

One night, after an early rather nice display of Northern Lights, I went into the Hi-Spot for coffee and to de-frost my glasses. When my "specs" had finished thawing, I looked up to see merry hazel-green eyes watching me. I knew him instantly.

His eyes were tender and laughing and saying, "There you are! I'm so glad to see you."

He smiled as he came over and sat down next to me. I was a little off-guard and tongue-tied, but almost without any control over my tongue I asked him: "Well, how's the bone structure of a bovine these days?"

He laughed merrily at that, throwing his head back and really laughing. Then, with a half-smile he said, "More like the bone structure of a moose every day!"

Soon we were chatting comfortably. I told him about my new job at the Pioneer Hotel coffee shop, and he talked a bit of the history of that place, which was apparently one of the oldest buildings in Fairbanks.

In our earlier conversation, neither of us had been really intro-duced, so I told him my name, using the now adopted nickname: "I go by Toni. What's yours?"

"Lester," he said, "Call me Les."

I laughed. "You're kidding! You look more like a 'Chuck.' Can I call you that?"

He laughed some more and told me, "I wouldn't answer to it so what's the use? To say it like Shakespeare, 'What's in a name?'"

For the first time in my life, I was meeting good men friends I could really talk to. Among the men who bolstered a young lost soul were Chuck, Les, and Fritz.

Alaska was a new world, a world that talked to a woman in her own terms. In those days, down in the "South 48" where I had come from before Alaska, it seemed to me that men always talked down to women. It was refreshing to feel comfortable talking about all sorts of things.

New adventures were everywhere. I told Les about trying to cook on the White Pass railway, and the trip over the new Alcan Highway. And about the drunk singing under our window that night in Fairbanks, and Nelda's new job in Valdez.

Les told me of a gold mining job he had lined up for the summer. "Gold mining was closed down during the war," he said, "because it wasn't a critical mineral, but now gold mining is going again." I told him that was one of the many Alaskan adventures I was seeking.

"I want to see some dog sledding and flying. I have never been up in an airplane."

He said, "If you want to fly, Weeks Field is just down the main drag. They will take people up for a short trip for very little cost.

He hesitated a bit, "It's pretty dark most of the time though, so go during daylight.

"If you want to ride in a dog sled, all you have to do is go out to the Army on a Saturday and ask if they'll take you out. They have to run the dogs almost every day to keep them in trim and to break in new sled dogs."

I talked about the howling of the Huskies that sound more like wolves than dogs. I said, "The way they sound is, well, just really savage!"

He agreed with me on that sound. "Yeah, I know that sound. Most dog teams are part wolf anyhow. Fairbanks still allows dog teams to be tethered inside the city limits. But I think it won't be that way very long, now that the war is over."

He looked at me a moment, "You really like a lot of things, don't you?"

I shrugged. "There are a lot of things I have never seen, and some of them I never heard of until now. I want to see and learn about Alaska."

I was beginning to realize that all of Alaska sort of "closed down" in the winter, but next spring was where it's at!

Already I was trying to be a writer, but I never really believed I could be one. If I was going to write, it wouldn't be fiction; I wanted the real "skinny," so to speak.

Over the next few months, I had many great conversations with both Lester and Fritz. We talked and talked. The one thing I treasure in any companion, male or female, is good conversation. Les and Fritz had that quality. Their interests ranged through hunting and fishing, to history, gold mining, dog sledding and the offbeat characters of early Alaska.

*Lone E. Janson*

But men talk differently when they are with other men, and women do the same. I still longed for the companionship of another girl near my own age, but it would be many months before I even met such a friend. In the meantime, it was the companionship of Fritz and Les that kept me in touch with my new world.

From both men, I learned a lot about Alaska. Between them, they made me feel the immediacy of frontier Alaska, and how it was possible to meet the very people that the mountains were named for. I got to know the real roots of the country.

One day Lester pointed out Cap Lathrop to me.

"That man is Alaska's only millionaire."

I looked at the man in the well-worn wool plaid shirt, the scuffed shoepacks and the slouch hat. He sure didn't look like any millionaire I ever heard of. But then, no other millionaire I ever heard of commanded the respect and affection Cap Lathrop did.

"He has done more to help the Territory than anyone else," Les told me. "Anyone else would have taken his money and left like all the other non-resident carpetbaggers, but not Cap. He has stayed here and reinvested it."

There was an unmistakable affection in his voice. I was to hear that in every Alaskan voice who ever talked about Cap over the years. Those were the days when Alaska had only one millionaire—and loved him.

Fritz sensed I was rather lost and lonely, so he hovered around me like a worried father. He took me to dances and visiting his friends, and we talked a great deal. There was so much to learn, the country so new, so wild and empty. The people who were here were often survivors of the Gold Rush itself. That thought filled me with awe, but Fritz knew many such people.

The conversations with Les were similar. When the weather was moderate we walked around. At other times we sat in the cafe and talked. A few times we went to his little tan house on Garden Island and sat over hot coffee exchanging experiences and ideas. I'd forget the time and the place and all else while we visited. Those were wonderful times, and I learned a lot about Alaska.

At all times both Les and Fritz were perfect gentlemen. I never knew if it was my tender age or the respect Alaska men seemed to accord all women, or a combination of the two factors. They were great friends to have during that lonely time.

I liked working at the Pioneer Coffee Shop, and appreciated the historic old hotel, but I had only worked there a few weeks when disaster struck. From my rented room I heard the fire horn blatting out its call to the Volunteer Fire Department, and followed the fire engines down to the Chena Slough in time to see the Pioneer Hotel wrapped in flames.

I was out of work again—in the middle of winter. The loss of this job with the Christmas season at hand was devastating.

Before the smoke cleared, I went to the little tan house on Garden Island to see my friend Les for comfort. Our visits had always cheered me up, but not this time.

It really hadn't occurred to me to wonder why all we ever did was talk; it just seemed so natural. I had an older brother, and I really thought of Les as someone like him. But this time Lester was very cool, and I was too young in any case. He wasn't about to start anything with me, jail bait. He looked on me, and treated me, like a kid sister. But now he felt it best to end the friendship.

I was stunned. I was too young, I guess, to have read the signs and seen it coming. I went out into the cold night and determined to stay away. In any case, I had a job to find.

How I wished I had a "best friend" to exchange girl talk with. That was the one thing I missed, since I had no family here in Alaska. It was always dark, contributing to my depression.

Someone mentioned jobs on the Army base at Ladd Field, so I went to a government office to apply for a job—any job I could find to get me through till spring when other work opened up.

It was here that I met another famous and respected old-time Alaskan. Except that I didn't know who he was. Again, here was a man dressed informally, and being friendly with one and all.

I had just come out of a back office from my job interview, where I had been hired to work in the Ladd Field laundry. I now had a job to last until spring and was feeling relieved and happy. The man, who was the center of attention, picked up my application blank and glanced at it.

He said, "It's a shame for someone with a good education like yours to have to work in a laundry."

I was a little puzzled. I didn't think a high school education was much. I had always thought in terms of college even though I knew that neither my mom nor myself could afford it, and that I probably never would have it, at least in a formal sense—that is, no sheepskin diploma. But I fully intended to keep studying on my own.

The moment passed, and someone else claimed the stranger's attention, asking where he had been and how the weather was. He laughed and said he had been in Seattle, looking for sunshine. I remembered vividly how little sunshine Seattle boasted in the winter, and how much rain.

I laughed and said, "You won't find much sunshine in Seattle, you jerk!" It had no meaning. It was the young people's slang of the day.

There was suddenly a sort of hush in the room, like everyone was holding their breath. The man who was the object of the jibe just laughed and the banter picked up again. As soon as he departed, one of the secretaries turned to me.

She said, "Do you know who that was?"

"No," I said.

"That was the governor of Alaska, Governor Ernest Gruening."

With my foot in my mouth, I went out to begin my new job.

# Chapter Nine

## SLATER CAMP

### Fairbanks—December 1945

Fairbanks was crawling with soldiers that winter of 1945-46, mostly southern boys, it seemed. These southern boys didn't seem to know how to handle themselves in Arctic climes. They walked around at 60-below in their fur caps with the earflaps up and their ears glowing cherry-red in the cold. Now I found myself in contact with the military side of Fairbanks, at least the civilian-military side of it, a new experience to me.

I reported for work at the Ladd Field laundry, and, as recommended by civilian employees, to Slater Camp for housing.

The superintendent of the camp, Marvin, was a jolly rotund man. He had a habit of saying "hm" whenever he was at a loss for words, which apparently was how I affected him most of the time.

He was very nice, understood my need for inexpensive housing and even loaned me twenty dollars, which in those days would buy food for several weeks in the cafeteria. It took me six months to pay him back, and when I did, all he said was "hm."

I liked Marvin very much in a fatherly sort of way, except for his matchmaking penchant. He decided early on that I needed to be married, and he knew just the right guy, a young truck driver friend of his.

I sort of hemmed and hawed when he suggested setting me up with a date with this fellow, and I got the keys to my room and escaped as quickly as I could.

Just like the room at Glacier Station, this one was Spartan in its simplicity. Instead of a cot, it had a bed, but Marvin had to lend me bedding. The window had no curtains, and I pinned a sheet across for the time being.

Then I went to work at the laundry. My boss was a bouncy and very popular young sergeant we called Jonesy. Sgt. Jonesy and I were close enough in age to eye each other with interest, and even to go out once or twice, but we never got beyond the dancing and not-too-serious flirting stage. The flirting was fun, though.

Slater Camp itself was an interesting experience, especially the mess hall. In those days the entire Territory of Alaska (over twice the size of Texas) had only three commercial radio stations, all owned by Cap Lathrop Enterprises. One of them was KFAR in Fairbanks. Every morning the cafeteria radio would be tuned to KFAR. The disk jockey was a zany panic called "Williwaw Willie." (A "williwaw" is a very sudden, violent gust of wind that dies out right after lifting your hat right off your head.) Williwaw Willie's delightful lunacy really brightened up our mornings as we went down the cafeteria line under the sign that read, "Take all you want, but eat all you take." Williwaw Willie had the cleverest, funniest line of patter I ever heard, perfect for offsetting the dreary cafeteria fare and the Army barracks ambiance. He was a bright morning spot in a life that I was finding more and more depressing as Christmas approached.

Just the thought of Christmas sent me into a deep blue funk that year, despite living in an Arctic wonderland that looked for all the world like a real-life Christmas card. Part of it may have been that it was always night, regardless of its beauty. Days were about two hours long, and I was at work then. It simply was always dark.

Fritz had gone Outside to visit friends, and I hadn't seen Lester since we parted ways. I had no close friends to talk to as the holidays approached. There was no TV in 1945, of course, and I didn't have a radio; only the one in the cafeteria was available to listen to, and the cafeteria wasn't open during the lonely late hours. Now I had no pleasant conversations with my only two close friends, and due to the lop-sided male-female ratio, I had no "best friend" to talk to. I was feeling lonely and lost. I especially missed Lester, and longed to just sit and talk as we had done before. I frequently walked past the little tan house, noting if the lights were on, and wishing I could drop in, or at least run into him in one of the coffee shops. I still walked a lot, more to get away from the Army camp and the empty drab room with the sheet across the window than anything else. I never tried to improve that room, not even to replace the sheet. It was simply too depressing.

Meanwhile, Marvin was busy promoting his hoped-for Big Romance with truck driver Jack as the Christmas season approached. I liked Jack well enough, but Marvin's matchmaking really didn't help us get along any better. Jack wasn't a great conversationalist, and I missed the visiting that I had enjoyed with Fritz and Lester. Jack and I went to a few dances, and he was a pleasant but dull companion and an indifferent dancer. Between us there was no spark at all.

But Marvin, encouraged because I went out with Jack on a few dates, kept busy arranging fascinating things that would throw us together. First he sent us out across the frozen tundra to cut a Christmas tree, which turned out to be fun. And so was the decorating party, although it consisted of only the three of us, and took place in my Army-barracks-type room in front of the sheet over the window. It was such a barren room with no signs of my own personal touch, because I felt nothing about it. Needless to say, the tree looked just about the same, I guess, because it left no lasting impression on me.

Marvin, unaware of the disenchantment of those around him, wangled an invitation for us to a combination wedding reception-Christmas Eve party that took place at the camp. He was vastly pleased. He beamed with satisfaction that Jack and I would be exposed to this matrimonial example. The word "party" was enough for me. I found myself almost looking forward to it in spite of Marvin's thinly veiled matchmaking. He kept making admiring remarks about newlyweds, no doubt hoping to inspire us.

One thing about Marvin, there wasn't a subtle bone in his body. You had to like the guy.

The party was not as much fun as I had hoped, not even as much fun as decorating my dismal tree had been. Jack and I stood on the fringes with nothing to say and no one to say it to. There was no dancing, and we were sort of lost. The newlyweds tended to gaze into each other's eyes and forget there were others there. Actually, I was glad that they were the center of attention. I didn't know anyone there, and apparently neither did Jack, and it was easy to quietly leave. We parted early, neither of us having anything to say nor any good ideas of what else to do. He walked me to my apartment door and said goodnight. I was glad we hadn't progressed to the kissing stage, because I simply wasn't in the mood.

I went inside, but I couldn't stand the quiet apartment. Some Christmas Eve this was! I had to get out. So I bundled up warmly and took a walk. Outside the night was clear and cold, with the moon gleaming on the snow. The fierce cold snatched at my nose and reached through my heavy woolen scarf to finger my ears. I blinked hard to protect my eyes, and the inside of my scarf was caked with ice from my breath. The steady squeak, squeak of mukluks marked my progress over the hard-packed snow.

The Arctic night was outdoing itself for sheer splendor. The stars sparkled with the unusual brilliance of a sub-zero temperature, and the moon flooded the white world with silver. Above it all, suspended like a fiery curtain, the Northern Lights burned, weaving and crackling in the clear night sky. It was like being in another world.

The piercing cold quickened my step and I cut across an open field. As I turned onto a path, I passed beneath a tree dripping icicle-diamonds in the moonlight.

I was aware of the sounds of the night: a branch creaking under its frosty load, the crunch of my own footsteps, and the plaintive howl of a distant Husky.

Suddenly I stopped, for now I could hear something else. Somewhere nearby a phonograph was playing. I had forgotten how sound carries in sub-zero temperatures. There was no way to know where it came from, but it was music: Christmas carols seemingly from nowhere, as if the angels were singing again on this Christmas Eve, my first in Alaska. A wave of homesickness washed over me and I blinked hard to hold back the tears.

I hunched down farther into my coat and began to walk fast. When I looked up, I was not really surprised to see where I was. There was Les' little tan house, a warm light showing through the window blinds. I strolled the length of the block and turned back, walking very slowly past. I wanted with every fiber of my being to walk up to the door and ring the bell, but I fought back that feeling. It was just Christmas Eve and I was lonely, I knew.

I jammed my hands deeply into my pockets and walked firmly away. I had my pride, after all. Besides, I was getting cold—darned cold—and I decided to head for home.

When I went into the hall at the camp, the party was just breaking up. People were leaving, and two girls were coming out. One was a married woman I knew from the laundry and the other I had seen somewhere, probably around the camp. She was blonde, with light brown eyes of an unusual color, and she was open and hearty, the perfect antidote for my own depression. The woman from the laundry introduced me to her. Her name was Marian Arnold, and we became fast friends before the winter was out.

"Come on," they urged. "We're going to a friend's house to finish the party!" And off we went, laughing and exchanging stories. What a lovely Christmas present: companionship of my own age and sex, the best present of all!

To my shock, when we got to the "friend's house," it was Les' little tan one. Les was gone. He had moved away some time earlier, and a new tenant was there. I didn't know whether I was relieved or sad at that news, but with such merry companions, who cared?

Marian was barely a year older than myself, but already a world traveler. She had stories of serving in the Swedish Merchant Marine as a crewmember on a freighter, and all sorts of travel yarns. It was what I needed to snap me out of my blue funk. From that night on, winter in Fairbanks became bearable again.

At the laundry, work was brisk through the Christmas season. But right after New Years it dropped off to almost nothing. We'd finish up our work rather early in the shift, and spend the rest of the day drinking coffee and telling jokes, or laying in laundry hampers, just gold-bricking in general. Jonesy and I flirted a little, but our hearts weren't in it. It was just a nice pastime.

One day Jonesy came running up and in a stage whisper alerted us all: "There's going to be a surprise inspection—get busy!" So we did. We jumped out of our comfortable laundry hampers and began piling laundry bundles in them. When the hamper was full, we'd start unloading them onto the shelves again, and when we finished that, the same bundles came down off the shelf once more. Boy, we were busy, hard-working folks while the brass made the rounds. As soon as they departed, it was gold-brick time again. I found the whole routine highly amusing.

I plunged into a frenzy of new adventures. It was the long shank of winter and it took imagination to think up things to do.

I remembered the dog sleds that Les had told me about. So Saturday found me swathed in my scarf, hiking out to the base where friendly guys at the gate pointed the way to the dog sled area.

*Lone E. Janson*

This was my first encounter with a dog sled. The day was clear and cold, with hardly a breath of wind, a typical winter day in Fairbanks. The days were still very short, about three hours long, but time enough for a brisk go-around in the sled. The lead dog on duty that day was a beautiful Husky named "Smokey." I watched the boys hitch up the team, admiring the intelligent looking lead dog.

They put me in the sled, and covered me with a smelly wolf-skin blanket. At first I recoiled from the odor, but when Smokey started his run and the eager dogs plunged down the trail after him, I began to feel the effects of wind chill from our speed. I was more than happy to snuggle down in that wolf-skin robe and never mind the smell.

What a thrill! We dashed down that narrow trail pell-mell, the dogs eager for the exercise and full of enthusiasm for the run. I thought there could never be anything so exciting, or cold, as a ride in a dog sled. The dogs' tails were all lifted happily and their love of running was totally evident.

All too soon we were back, the sergeant pointing out that it would soon be dark, and he couldn't keep me out on the trail too long. But he said I could come back next Saturday, but come earlier and we'd have a longer ride. I went home glowing from the fabulous adventure.

Next Saturday I was back, but the Army had other uses for Smokey, and there were no lead dogs available. The guys must have seen my disappointment, so they said, well, there's a young potential lead dog still in training here. Why don't we hitch her up and give her a try? That sounded fine to me.

The boys hitched up the team, led by the unseasoned lead dog. They took the sled out empty the first time, before I was to ride. The lady lead dog followed and worked faithfully as long as the handler held her collar and ran alongside. When he let go, she spun around, upsetting the sled and snarling the harnesses and running like sixty for home. The sled bounced drunkenly along on its side. It was then I began to realize why dog drivers have so much affection for true lead dogs.

Nevertheless, the boys thought we might try it again, and he'd hang onto her longer. So into the reeking wolf-skin I snuggled and off we went. It was the same story, except that I was in the sled. As soon as he let go of her collar, into the snow bank I went, and off for home she went, the sled crashing along behind. I came up laughing and spitting snow out of my mouth, and we all mushed merrily back and gave it one more try. After another go at it, and another dump in the snow, we all decided to call it quits.

I said I'd come back when Smokey was there. And so I did, a number of times that winter. I still have a copy of Josephine Crumrine's painting of Smokey and treasure the memory of the good times I had with him in the lead. Even the smell of the wolf-skin robe doesn't seem so bad in retrospect.

Another adventure I sought out was flying. I had never been up in a plane, though I had dreamed of learning to fly since my early teens. I became so caught up in other adventures that it just hadn't happened.

One day I wandered out to Weeks Field there in Fairbanks. At that time it was the city airport. There were a few hangars scattered along the strip, and a couple of mechanics doing some desultory work on a plane or two.

I went up to one and asked how I could get a plane ride. He pointed his wrench in the direction of a nearby hangar and informed me I could go up for about ten or fifteen minutes for ten dollars. I was delighted, and went right over. One of the pilots in the hangar set down his coffee and took my money. Then he went out and warmed up the plane. I crawled in, all a-tingle. The plane roared down the runway, and suddenly the roughness of its passage smoothed right out—we were airborne! It was a great feeling. I wonder if everyone remembers her or his first lift-off as vividly as I remember mine. Of course, I think it is more exciting in a small plane like the one I went up in, and on a gravel strip such as Weeks Field.

I was hooked on flying after that, even though all I did was ride along. I went out to the field often just to talk to the pilots. Most of them were pretty busy and didn't have much time for me, but they liked to have someone around who radiated enthusiasm for flying.

Gradually the winter was slipping by. A curling rink was built near the courthouse, and the new sport of curling was introduced. I watched a few times as the brooms were used to coax the what-cha-ma-call-it across the ice. There was a winter carnival early in the year, and the parade was fun.

One day I got a letter from my mother telling me she was going into surgery within the week, and would I be able to come home and stay with her for a while? My brother was still in the Navy, stationed aboard the USS Missouri, and so she was alone.

There were some new air routes coming on line since the war was over. Pan American was one flying south from Fairbanks. The trip would take twelve hours, perhaps more, with all sorts of stops for fuel, but it sounded a whole lot shorter than the boat trip of six days, plus the train ride of two more days.

I was worried about Mom, so I quickly packed and made arrangements for the flight home on Pan American World Airways.

I flew different airlines each way on that trip, each flying along a different side of the mountains so I could see and experience more. What I remember most vividly about these flights are the contrasts. The Coast Range of Southeast Alaska is a continuation of the Rocky Mountains that stretch clear down to the Andes of South America. They are like the backbone of the continents. Pan American flew on the Pacific Ocean side of the Coast Range. On my return trip north I flew Canadian Pacific on the opposite side of that range. No geography lesson in the world could put the continent into perspective with a more powerful visual impression.

During the southern leg, the world ended at the high rocky barrier of the mountains. Below me was a marine world, that same island-mountain paradise I had sailed through in August the previous year. The mountains formed the eastward barrier, and the Pacific Ocean spread out endlessly to the west. Coming back, the same mountains formed the same barrier, but on the west. To the east spread the immense Great Plains as far as the eye could see. How BIG was the world on both sides!

The season changes were to present another contrast. When I left Fairbanks it was winter and a time of cold and darkness. When I returned it was summer, a time of dusty, suffocating heat, mosquitoes, and constant daylight. The daylight I enjoyed.

The previous winter, while I had been waiting for the plane in Fairbanks to go home to see my mother, the season was far enough advanced that the days had begun to lengthen at last. It was daylight when I took off, a remarkable change all by itself. The temperature was not all that cold, maybe 13 below, but for the first time that winter, there was a slight breeze. That tiny stirring of the air subjected me to the first wind chill factor of the winter. It felt colder than it ever had at -40 degrees. The telephone wires where the snow had remained undisturbed throughout the winter suddenly were cleared of snow by the knife-edge slice of the wind.

That flight south on Pan Am gave me a chance to appreciate more fully the beauty of the marine coast that I had seen from the deck of the steamship. The water sparkled green-blue between the myriad islands, and I had a new view of the glaciers tumbling from the mountains. Even though there was snow on the ground, all was basically green because of the evergreen forests.

Then I was home. The next couple of months were a kaleidoscope of activity as my mother went through her operation and recovery, and I found work in a restaurant in Vancouver, Washington, and began saving money to go back to Alaska. As winter waned I became more and more restless. Spring really gave me itchy feet. Life here "Outside," after Alaska, was so drab and meaningless. Nobody, it seemed, had an ounce of adventure or individualism in them. In Alaska, everyone did, and I couldn't wait to return.

*Lone E. Janson*

# Chapter Ten

## FLIP SIDE OF FAIRBANKS

### Spring 1946

The months of work to garner enough money to return to Alaska seemed endless. I counted every paycheck and squeezed every nickel till the buffalo bellowed, and eventually I made it. I still had the penny in my shoe, but I have to admit it was a different penny. They were the same shoes, though.

I had chosen to return on Canadian Pacific Air because adventure and gathering experiences was the goal, and this would offer a different route and new vistas. I would ride the ferry from Seattle to Victoria, B.C., and thence to Vancouver, B.C., where I'd catch the plane north to Fairbanks.

When I boarded the ferry in Seattle, there was a brisk, chilly wind blowing on Puget Sound, so I dressed warmly in a wool suit with a woolen sweater underneath.

The first stop was Victoria, B.C., which was a taste of Old England, quaint and charming, and very friendly. The ferry was met by a Scottish bagpipe troupe clad in kilts, and those vivid melodies skirling across the water made the spine tingle. A ship approaching shore is a thing of beauty, especially when met in such special fashion.

The ferry landed in Vancouver, B.C., in plenty of time to make connections with the plane. The DC-3 warmed up, and roared off into the night. As was the custom, the stewardess came around with a pillow and a blanket, and a stick of gum to chew to relieve ear pressure problems. Ear pressure, noise, and draftiness were the big drawbacks of air travel in those days, even though the DC-3 was a quiet airplane by the standards of the time. Still, carrying on a conversation in a DC-3 was something of a challenge, just as it had been on the Alcan Highway bus.

Darkness fell soon after leaving Vancouver, B.C. Off to the left the mountains stood out clear and sharp in the ghostly moonlight. They rose white and jagged from the black void of forest below. For a distance you could mark the lonely road, the infant Alaska (Alcan) Highway, by the progress of a single car in the night. The only other thing to see was an occasional feeble glimmer of light where some lonely trapper still read by Blazo lamplight.

Along about midnight we made a stop at Ft. St. John, deplaning for a delicious midnight breakfast of hot cakes with honey, eggs, bacon and steaming coffee at the local café. The meal done, several of us went outside to enjoy the night air and to watch a breathtaking display of Northern Lights. It was one of the most beautiful I had ever seen, and I considered myself a connoisseur by that time.

Then once more we were in the air, following the route of the World War II "air ferry." It was the same route used during World War II by hundreds of planes that were sent to Russia by this route under a "Lend-Lease" program to fight Nazi Germany. We stopped at Watson Lake and, I think, Northway to refuel. The short range of the DC-3 was the reason all the new airfields were built along the route of the Alcan Highway.

Back in the plane, I was so happy to be heading back to Alaska that I was all choked up. The months it had taken me to earn my way back had seemed almost interminable. I now felt truly a stranger in what had been my home country in the South 48. Finally, I was on my way back to Alaska.

Outside the airplane window it was becoming light. Glancing at my watch I saw that it was only 2 a.m.! We were actually flying INTO DAYLIGHT as we flew north! I was fascinated as the sky brightened, then the tundra below became a soft downy green, and finally the sun itself peeped, then popped, over the rim of the world by three in the morning. I had never heard of such hours for sunrise. Remember, I had only been half a year in Alaska, experiencing only the long, depressing darkness of winter. Now, without any warning or real preparation, I was seeing the opposite side of the coin.

During the next five hours between snoozes I looked at the snake-like paths of rivers across the tundra, and watched small, heavy clouds crawl over the hills to spill in the crevasses between. On my right stretched the vast level continent of the Canadian prairies. Beneath me was a marvelous glimpse of millions of muskeg ponds on the vivid green tundra, and the sinuous windings of unnamed rivers of the north. On the left rose the stark white pinnacles of the Coast Range of mountains.

On the other side of those mountains was Southeast Alaska, I knew. On the right was Canada, as far as the eye could see.

Later, with my ears tired and ringing from the constant noise of the DC-3 engines, suddenly we were over Ladd Field in Fairbanks. Then I was climbing out to be assaulted by shimmering heat and a fighter squadron of well-armed mosquitoes. I cursed myself for wearing a wool suit and sweater to this sub-tropical clime. It was a hot miserable wait for my bags and a long ride into town. As we pulled up to the Nordale Hotel, there was a bank sign that showed the temperature—it was over 90 degrees! And only eight in the morning! But of course up here the sun had been up since about 1 a.m., so there had been seven hours of warm sunshine to heat things up. I hadn't been prepared for the heat of a Fairbanks summer.

In my room, I almost ripped the heavy woolen clothes off my body, trying to get some relief from the heat. A cool shower, then down to the coffee shop for some lemonade, and I was ready to go out and see Fairbanks in the summer.

What I was to remember the most about Fairbanks in the summer was the dust. It rose from the unpaved streets in yellow choking clouds, yellow from sunlight, not from its own intrinsic color. It was kind of fun, though, to walk around Fairbanks streets at one or two in the morning in broad daylight. There were people up and around at all hours. It was as if Alaskans forgot about time. You worked when there was work to do, played as long as you felt like it, slept when sleepy. No stores were open in the middle of the night, but folks were out on the streets visiting with one another anyway.

Over the next few days, I learned to forget all I thought I knew about the sun rising in the east and setting in the west. What it did here was rise in the north at about one a.m., perform a huge circle around the sky, and set again in the north at about eleven p.m. This circle-around-the-sky concept defied all I had ever learned or experienced. I found out that later in the year from a high mountain or just a little further north, it did not set at all—just made a full circle around the sky.

At "night" the mosquitoes came out in force to enjoy the brief cool twilight, although there was no true "darkness" at all. The mosquitoes didn't go away when the sun came up, but they just came out stronger and more bloodthirsty in the cooler hours. There were also little black

*Lone E. Janson*

gnats that loved the hot weather, flies, and particularly vicious little villains called "no-see-ums." To this tiny villain, window screens had no meaning at all. They went right through them, and when they bit, you HAD to go get them. Oh, and the bane of berry-pickers everywhere, the biting flies called "white sox." I have never seen one, but my ankles have fallen prey to them many times. When they bite (preferring the tender ankle area), they take a big chunk of flesh out and leave an itchy, burning crater. Lovely little bugs.

Oh well, that's just part of summer in Alaska. The warm, lo-o-ong summer days more than made up for it. Flowers simply burst from the ground and bloomed with a joyous vigor, and the farming was a joy to behold because of the long growing days: all day and all night too.

I had a lot of new impressions to absorb during the next few days. I also had a job to find, and someone at the hotel told me to go see Lulu Fairbanks, Fairbanks' official, unofficial greeter of new people.

Lulu was rather elderly at that time; at least she looked so to my young eyes. I thought she would have a heart attack when I told her my story: I had just arrived back in Alaska and was looking for work. She gasped and choked, and then launched into a long tirade that caught me off-guard.

"Do you mean to tell me you came up to Alaska without a job?" she demanded. "How could you have done such a thing? What were you thinking of? Why, NO ONE comes to Alaska without a job..." and on and on. I watched this performance for a few minutes in a state of shock. I hadn't had a chance to get a word in edgewise. But when I had the chance, I told her what she wanted to hear, that I still had a job at the Ladd Field laundry if I wanted it, but I was looking for waitress work... blah, blah, blah. I don't know if I could have gone back to work at Ladd Field or not. I had no intention of trying for the job, but Lulu was mollified. She really was a nice woman. I think it was simply the "gypsy girl" thing again. Lots of people seemed to have trouble with that in the mid-forties. I got used to these people, and learned quickly how to deal with them. I made my escape from Lulu as soon as possible because I could see she would be no help.

In any case I knew how to proceed. I started going into cafes and asking the managers if they needed a waitress, a good waitress. It was at the very first cafe where I asked that question that I landed a job. The owner asked how much experience I had, and I told him. He said to be there next morning at 6 a.m. After all, it was now summer in Alaska and jobs were plentiful.

The next morning I reported about 5:30 a.m. so I could eat before starting my shift, and I had a bowl of cereal in front of me when the owner let in the first customer—before opening time. Well, okay. I got up and waited on him, then went back to finish my oatmeal. The owner decided then and there that I had lied about being experienced, but he didn't say anything to me. Instead, the next day or so I overheard him telling one of the customers that I had failed to pick up my dishes and quit eating when the first customer came in, so he knew I had lied about my waitress experience. I don't like making a scene, so I waited for a quiet time on shift to go over and quit. I told him I'd finish the shift but I was through, that he could call me a bum waitress anytime, but never to call me a liar. He had the grace to look embarrassed, and paid me without giving me a bad time (which hasn't always been my experience).

So there I was again. Oh well, it wasn't much of a job anyway. I tucked the meager paycheck in my pocket, checked the penny that still rode in my shoe, and went out into the cloud of yellow dust with a dejected air. I didn't seem to be having very good luck with my Alaskan jobs.

I was walking along, not sure where I was going or what to do next, when I heard a horn honking. I looked up to see a pickup truck on the street, and the man behind the wheel honking wildly. It was Fritz Larson.

He was just beside himself to see me, and I was very happy to find an old friend again. We drove someplace to have coffee and talk. When he heard my story about the cafe job, he said not to worry he had a job for me. He asked if paint smells bothered me, and I told him no, so he hired me to work in his little carpentry and woodworking shop as a painter.

I rather enjoyed the work of painting. I didn't know much about this work, so I simply enjoyed what I did. What it boiled down to mostly was staining and varnishing stools. I love wood and I enjoy seeing its beauty come to vibrant life with the application of a proper finish. I was as careful with the stools as if they were my own, working all the crossties and underpinnings as carefully as the seat and other more visible parts. They came out as beautiful stools, so I was happy.

Meanwhile, I had launched once more into the happy pursuit of adventure. I went out to Weeks Field to talk to the flyboys and mechanics again and just to be around the small airplanes.

One of the fellows was checking out his plane prior to takeoff. I watched the process and helped him a little whenever he needed another hand with something.

The pilot was Ted Rasmussen and he was preparing for a flight out to see an old sourdough in the Bush. Most pilots appreciate another set of eyes in the cockpit, so he asked me if I wanted to come along. I jumped at the chance. After correcting his flight plan, we took off into the bright summer sky.

About half an hour later we were circling a small cabin near a tiny dirt strip. A man came out and waved, Rasmussen waggled his wings, and then came in for a landing. After unloading the groceries and supplies the man wanted, we were invited into the cabin for boiled coffee and Mulligan stew.

The roof of the old-timer's log cabin was covered with soil, and it was a riot of color: pansies, forget-me-nots, daisies and other wild flowers bloomed there. Inside, under that garden-roof, we drank strong boiled coffee and talked while the sourdough massaged Olga's ears lovingly. This was what Alaska was about, I thought—a dog named Olga, Mulligan stew and a garden on the roof.

The next weekend Fritz Larson asked me if I wanted to go fishing for grayling with him. That sounded like a great adventure, even though I had never seen a grayling. He had an extra pole and he brought along some worms as bait. We drove up the Steese Highway north of Fairbanks on this trip, where I saw some different kinds of mountains. These mountains were just as high and rugged as those along the coast, but they were geologically older mountains and did not have the sharp, pointed peaks of the Coast Range Mountains. They were smoothly rounded, and I was trying to fit this new type of mountain range into what I had been reading in my geology books.

As we drove along the highway, I particularly remember the roses. Wild roses bloomed absolutely everywhere, lovely pink rose blossoms alongside the road, with a heavenly scent. Their single rose blooms reminded me of the wild yellow rose bushes I had known and loved in Denver as a child.

We stopped at a lodge somewhere up the Steese. The proprietor of the lodge was a friend of Fritz's, and we had a nice visit that evening, talking about the next day's fishing.

In the morning we went out to try our luck in a nearby stream. I had really never been sport fishing, so I took a worm and was holding it uncertainly, asking Fritz how you got this thing on the hook? I didn't think anything of it, but Fritz got a big kick out of it. He had expected me to squeal and pull away from "those slimy things." He told this story to anyone who would listen in the lodge that evening, to my acute embarrassment.

During the afternoon's fishing I caught one very small grayling, and Fritz caught several, so we had grayling for supper. The small trout-like fish had a large dorsal fin that was its trademark, and they were delicious.

We were in the lobby visiting, and Fritz went out to take care of his fishing gear or something. The lodge owner took me aside and asked me how I was enjoying the trip. I told him the truth: it was wonderful. He asked about Fritz, and I told him of my admiration and friendship for Fritz. Then he just about blew my mind with the next remark.

"Why don't you grab that gink?"

Those were his exact words. I was puzzled, but failed to take any warning from the comment. I considered Fritz a good friend and I enjoyed being with him, but had never thought of him romantically. He seemed too old for me.

Fritz came back in, and we finished up a wonderful evening and went to our rooms. The next day we drove home, and Fritz asked me out to dinner and perhaps a dance. We had a fine time, and he took me to his place afterward for coffee. While we talked, Fritz proposed to me. I still hadn't digested the "grab that gink" remark when this happened. I was taken aback, and all I could do was stammer out my rejection of the offer. I hated to see how I had hurt a good friend, and I felt if I had been a little older, I might have seen it coming and either avoided it or softened it somehow. As it was, I had lost a good friend over romance.

I wasn't yet ready for marriage. Stricken, I wanted to move on, to get away from the heat and dust of Fairbanks. I had been thinking that what I wanted was an out-of-town summer job, and Fritz's proposal hastened the decision to seek one. Fritz maintained his usual gentlemanly demeanor and helpfulness as I made my preparations to move on.

I went over to Garden Island heading for the Alaska Road Commission office to ask about an out-of-town waitress job at one of the camps. I stopped in a small restaurant for coffee, and there I ran into Marian Arnold again. We squealed and hugged and all the things we do when we meet an old friend. Then we went to her apartment and sat up till after midnight, exchanging stories of our adventures and experiences.

We discussed what was next, and she said she was finishing up a job here in Fairbanks and had another one waiting in Barrow, so she'd be leaving soon for the farthest north town in Alaska. As we talked, I told her how I had seen a picture of Cordova, and that I had halfway decided that was the next place I'd like to see, but that I thought I'd try for a summer job in the Bush first. Marian was enchanted with the Cordova idea; she liked that one. If she hadn't already taken the job in Barrow, she would have come with me. I guess she was the catalyst for my Cordova trip.

The next day I wandered into the O'Harra Bus Lines office in the Nordale Hotel, mostly out of curiosity, and asked about the bus fare to Valdez, and the subsequent plane fare to Cordova. The price of a bus ticket was $21.15 to Valdez and another $10 or so for plane fare from Valdez to Cordova, which had no road. I had to allow $5 to overnight in Gakona, and maybe another $5 for meals along the way. As usual, I recorded these prices along with my daily adventures in my journal.

Marian was encouraging to the point of envy. She said "I know that's what I would do if I were at loose ends right now." Of course, she was committed to the Barrow job, so was not really free to go where she pleased just then.

There followed a flurry of preparations so I could be ready to leave with the bus the very next day.

# Chapter Eleven

## RICHARDSON HIGHWAY

### June 1946

It was June 15, 1946, the last day of my 18th year. Tomorrow, on my 19th birthday, I would be somewhere on the road, seeking new adventure.

I woke Marian early, but she was tired after putting in a full day plus four hours overtime the night before. I could only whisper "goodbye" as I left. I knew that tired feeling; I was a waitress. I went down to eat alone before starting out.

The bus was of the same type and vintage as I had taken from Whitehorse. There was some delay in getting started. An Indian man got on with his dog, but the driver said the dog had to be crated. The Indian went out to hunt up a crate without success. So he had to leave the dog. "I sure hate to lose that dog," he said sadly, shaking his head as we pulled away. I felt badly for both the Native and his dog, knowing by then the value of a good dog in Alaska.

Off we went, engulfed in the roar of shifting gears and the rattle of the bus over the gravel road, trailing its cloud of yellow dust.

The first 75 to 100 miles was through the tundra, rolling marshy land with stands of birch and spruce.

We had a breakfast stop at Richardson Roadhouse, where we ate again. The first rule of travel in those days was to eat at every opportunity, because you never knew how long before you might have another meal. The next roadhouse might not be open. (Unlike the Alcan, at least the Richardson Highway had roadhouses at regular stops.) You might break down and wait hours for help to come along. You might tangle with a moose or even a buffalo and come off second best. Or in winter you might get caught in, or between, avalanches. The possibilities were endless and the country was big and empty.

I have gone as long as 18 hours between meals while traveling in early Alaska, just because of such unforeseen circumstances. In those days you always ate whenever the opportunity offered, and a brown bag with a spare sandwich was a good insurance policy.

*Lone E. Janson*

At Richardson Roadhouse I had oatmeal, ham and eggs, spuds, toast and coffee, but was appalled that it cost a whole $1.75! As expensive as I thought meals were in Fairbanks, I had forgotten to allow for the added expense along the highway. At that rate, it would cost me more than my $5 for the two-day trip! I fingered my remaining few dollars and resolved to be more frugal for the rest of the trip. Fortunately, I carried a sandwich and candy bar in a brown bag for later.

From Big Delta we started climbing. We were in the foothills now and the Alaska Range was ahead. The only vegetation seemed to be a scrubby sort of wiry brush, gnarled and bent by the strong wind that blew constantly. I noticed quite a few gophers along the way; that's what I recorded in my journal, but I think they were marmots, or "whistlers."

Here and there repairs were being made on the road, and we made rough detours. Often a 'dozer had to go to work and improvise a road for us to pass. These were activities of the Alaska Road Commission, which Alaskans affectionately called the "Road Commotion."

It was the style in early Alaska to nickname everyone and everything. A nickname was frequently (not always) a sign of special respect and/or affection. In the case of the Alaska Road Commission (ARC), it was respect.

In those days, Alaska labored under discriminatory treatment on a number of fronts, especially concerning highways. There was even a landmark decision in the Supreme Court that said it was perfectly okay to discriminate against Alaska, because it was just a Territory. This was despite the fact that Alaska paid full highway taxes, but unlike the other Lower 48 states, it got very little back. These were the pauper years in Alaska. The ARC actually achieved minor miracles with the meager funds they had.

At one time along the road, we came to a dead stop because a pipe was being laid across the highway. At the side of the road the men were lying down resting. It was their lunch hour. No one moved to fix the road so we just sat there until they were through with their lunch break and good and ready to fix it. None of us groused about it; it was an accepted part of Alaskan life. After all, we had today and another full day of travel to get to Valdez, so what was the hurry? Let the guys eat their lunch in peace.

A little farther along we crossed a rise and abruptly pulled to a stop by the side of the road. The driver pointed out three big buffalo. A passenger grabbed a camera and took pictures while the shaggy beasts, as if sensing this, struck a perfect pose.

The driver said, "Fifty head of buffalo had been brought here from New York in 1923. The last count just before the war numbered 450. I think there are about 600 now."

I was sorry I didn't have a camera of my own on this trip.

The next stop was a ten-minute rest stop at Rapids Hunting Lodge, within a quarter of a mile of Black Rapids Glacier. I was amazed at the number of roadhouses. I chuckled that on the "Outside," a roadhouse meant a place to drink and dance, but here in Alaska the same name meant a lodge, a place for food, drink and comfortable rooms for the night, not to mention great conversation around a roaring fire in the lobby fireplace.

What a contrast the Richardson was to the Alcan! Until just before World War II, the Richardson was the only main highway in Alaska. It had been built as a military trail during the Gold Rush, improved to a horse and wagon trail in 1906. The first automobile successfully navigated this rude "highway," and there had been little real improvement since.

The most notable exception was during World War II. Up to that time, Thompson Pass into Valdez had never opened before the Fourth of July.

During the war they needed that road, so Al Ghezzi with his Alaska Freight Lines showed the bureaucrats that Thompson Pass could be kept open in the winter, and thereafter traffic could move at all times of the year, with the ARC making it possible.

But for me, the big contrast was between this highway and the fledgling "Alcan" Highway. The Richardson was an established "highway," with many roadhouses. On the Alcan, a "rest stop" was a convenient clump of bushes. The only "roadhouses" that I remembered were Burwash Landing, Champagne, and Northway.

After we left Black Rapids we were in the heart of the mountains. We followed the Delta River through Isabella Pass, named for the first woman through there, Isabella Barnette, a member of the first party to blaze the trail through the mountains.

*Lone E. Janson*

We passed Summit and Paxson Lake and soon were following the Gulkana River. From my brown bag I broke out a sandwich and a candy bar to eat along the way.

Sourdough Roadhouse was the next rest stop, where the lady called ahead to Santa Claus Lodge for meals and rooms. The crank-up "whoop-and-holler" telephone line operated on a line that was a converted section of the old military telegraph line dating from 1898. I knew the distance to Santa Claus Lodge was 22 miles because the wintertime dog races were held from Gulkana to Sourdough Roadhouse and back, a round trip of 44 miles. But on the old Richardson Highway, twenty-two miles was a good hour's drive, even if the road was in "good" condition.

I was very happy when we pulled into Santa Claus Lodge at Gulkana. It had been over twelve hours since we left Fairbanks, including rest and meal stops along the way. We were a well-worn group of travelers.

I shared a room with two ladies who were a lot of fun to be around. They were from California and heading for Anchorage over the new Glenn Highway. What fascinated me was that they had taken the riverboat down the Yukon River to Dawson, the trip I had been unable to make. They were excited and full of stories of their adventures and I listened avidly as they described the sternwheeler voyage to the Klondike. Even though they were much older than myself, they were truly kindred souls.

We had supper here and I had plenty of time to look around. There were lots of Indians here, and I walked a short distance down the road to admire a particularly beautiful dog team.

To the left of us, three mountains shared prominence: Mt. Sanford, Mt. Drum, and at a greater distance, Mt. Wrangell, an active volcano which had steaming craters at the top. From where I stood I could see four mountain ranges: the Alaska Range to the north, to the east the Wrangells, southward it was the Coast Range, and southwest the Chugach.

I slept that night surrounded by this grandeur.

On June 16, I woke to an absolutely beautiful 19th birthday, with Mt. Wrangell steaming happily away to the south of us. It reminded me of the feathery plumes of steam given off by the whales on my voyage north.

One of the ladies wished me a happy birthday so abruptly that we all had to laugh.

The ladies must have realized I was on short rations. They insisted they be allowed to treat me to a hearty breakfast for my birthday. Boy, I really ate well that morning: ham and eggs and fruit, and so on. I ate with a happy, young appetite, and thanked them for their birthday present of food.

They were such wonderful ladies, I was sorry to know that they were now going off on another direction. They were headed for Anchorage along a different bus over the brand new Glenn Highway to that town.

Now I was the only woman aboard, and I found that all the passengers except the driver and myself were Indians on that leg of the trip to Copper Center. I would have liked to talk to the Indian passengers. But I was too bashful to talk to them, and in any case the bus was too noisy for conversation.

Most of the Indians got off at the next stop, Copper Center. While there a tall blond fellow named George Peterson joined us. During rest stops we became good friends. Most visiting took place at rest stops; it still was too noisy on the bus. George worked for the "Road Commotion." He was used to this stuff.

One of our stops was at Tonsina Lodge, a long red two-story building with a sort of glassed-in area all around it. George told me that it was one of the old barracks from Fort Liscum near Valdez. The barracks building had been taken down to lumber and brought over Thompson Pass on the old Richardson Highway by horses and wagons.

I mentioned to him about the baby flattop Liscomb Bay and our short stint aboard it before the ship went off to war, only to be sunk by a Japanese torpedo. This was a fairly long rest stop, and George went into the kitchen to talk to friends he knew.

By this time the trip was beginning to seem very long, so I picked up a comic book on the coffee table and began reading. I almost fell asleep there. When I realized the bus was already loading, I came running out, hollering, "Here I am, the tail end of everything!" They kidded me for the rest of the trip about that.

I had a map on which I was trying to identify everything. I was sure the narrow river gorge we passed through was Thompson Pass. But it

*Lone E. Janson*

wasn't. I still hadn't realized how big Alaska is, and how bad the roads were.

We stopped at Tiekel for lunch. This place was nothing like the other roadhouses at which we stopped. It wasn't a sturdy log building with rooms for rent, like an inn. It was a small wood frame building almost like a cabin. That same little cabin was still there when I passed it in 1984, except that someone was adding another room.

I thought we were much closer to Valdez because of the Thompson Pass error, so I elected to eat dinner when I got to town—a mistake as I've pointed out before. I should have known better, but the meal would cost $1.50 and I knew I could get a square meal in Valdez for a dollar. As you can well imagine, my $5 budget was running very thin by now.

Instead of eating, I went out back to the shore of Tiekel River. Here I saw glacier silt along the riverbank where it settled out. I had an interest in geology and mineralogy even then, and I was fascinated by this detail.

Beyond Tiekel we started climbing to dizzy heights. We passed timberline and still were on the upgrade. We passed Worthington Glacier, a very picturesque river of ice, and kept on climbing.

Soon even the scrubby bushes of the type at Big Delta were left behind. Up here at these puritanical heights big boulders wore necklaces of ice. The only vegetation was a hardy form of moss which contrived to stay green where little pools of ice lay in depressions on the granite, and in the shelter of the rocks its blooms were absurdly large for the size of the plant, white flowers close to an inch across. Despite the sparse greenery I noticed more than one "whistler" (marmot). I found myself wondering what they ate.

Up here on the heights of Thompson Pass the road wound its way over scoured rock. Here and there small rivulets cut across, and just a bit of gravel filled them in. I thought it memorable because in essence it was already paved; the road was a well-worn path over solid rock winding over the high alpine summits. Of course it wasn't as level and smooth as a modern paved highway, but it certainly was a durable "pavement." At the top of Thompson Pass, the driver paused and pointed down into an immense canyon. Far below, we saw the road, hardly a tiny zigzag line. "That's where we're going," he said.

Then began the steep descent. Down we went; later I was to learn about this infamous "Three Mile Hill." It still had emergency upgrades here and there for runaway trucks. (An "upgrade" meant a turnout that turned uphill, to help slow down runaway trucks.)

Far below I saw a bridge across the river and a tunnel through solid rock, just where the river entered a narrow, steep-walled canyon, which the driver identified as Keystone Canyon.

But the driver pointed out that the tunnel was not yet finished, but was still under construction. On this trip we would be going across the old trail on the mountainside above Keystone Canyon. I got glimpses of it ahead, circling around, clinging to the edge of the cliff and crossing an exceptionally dirty, small glacier.

We were making our precarious descent, the bus in low gear and roaring loudly. When we got closer I could see that we were taking the high, rough road along the mountainside.

George worked with the Alaska Road "Commotion," but farther up north on other projects, still he was very interested. He began to ask questions of the driver about this new construction going on down in the lower reaches of the canyon. The driver described a particular "fill" which seemed to be one of the ARC's chief headaches. It seems that a blast of dynamite had been too powerful and the tunnel was condemned, so they tried to build around it.

The driver told George, "Now they are trying to remove the loose rock here and in other places. They have spent a whole season on it and still the rock is coming down. Now they don't know what they're going to do with it."

As we crawled along the road circling high above Keystone Canyon, we passed between two halves of a tiny, dirty hanging glacier. It was a recurring headache for the Road Commotion. It was a deep gully filled with moving snow and ice that each year took out whatever bridge had been built over that spot. It was easier to simply blast this small glacier in two where they wanted the road, and I assumed they did this whenever the glacier moved and grew together again. We came so near I could easily have reached out and touched the ice. It was a good ten feet high, and arched right over our heads above. The mountain was straight down on the other side. It was the perfect setting for freak accident tales about going over the edge.

*Lone E. Janson*

This area is now called the "Goat Trail" or the "Old Horse and Wagon Trail." I feel very privileged to have ridden over it the last year it was in use, on my nineteenth birthday!

Across the canyon a beautiful feathery waterfall tumbled down. It was Bridal Veil Falls, and it was flanked by other lovely cataracts whose beauty was overshadowed by this queenly cascade.

The waterfall I did not see was the one on our own side of the canyon—Horsetail Falls. We crossed the upper reaches above where it took its tumble down the rocks.

After that, about an hour's uneventful driving brought us into Valdez. We had descended from 2,722 feet at Thompson Pass to sea level in a distance of about twenty-five miles. On the last ten or twelve miles it was gravel moraine covered by the tallest cottonwood and spruces I had seen since Southeast Alaska.

A growling from my stomach reminded me how I had decided at Tiekel not to eat. It had taken nearly four hours to travel the tortuous Richardson from Tiekel (at Mile sixty-some) snaking up and over Thompson Pass, down above Keystone Canyon and across the glacier moraine flats to Valdez.

I was very, very hungry as we drove into Valdez at last.

# Chapter Twelve

## WAITING IN VALDEZ

### June 1946

Valdez was a sleepy little place built on one street. The bus made its way down a quiet boulevard to the Golden North Hotel where we were to stay. George got off the bus while I was gathering up my few belongings, yawning and stretching.

It had been a long day from Santa Claus Lodge in Gulkana over the pass to Valdez, a stretch that nowadays can be made in a couple of hours—if you like to drive leisurely and take in a few stops to enjoy the majestic scenery.

At that time I had no such perspective. I was tired. I was hungry. I was sorry that I hadn't eaten at Tickel, but it would have just about taken all the loose money I had. I still kept those few War Bonds in case of trouble. But I was surviving, and I was almost to Cordova!

Wearily, I carried my few bags into the hotel and came up behind George, who was talking to the manager. They were obviously old friends. I was sleepily wondering where, and whether, I would eat tonight.

The manager asked, "And is this the little woman?"

My surprise and consternation left me speechless, and George was about the same. A moment of surprise, then we both laughed. The incident had its up side; it woke me up enough to eat a sandwich at a small cafe before turning in.

Early the next day I met George in the lobby, and we went to see a Mr. Burch to learn when the plane would come. George was going to Cordova for an "old home week" with friends.

I was beginning to understand that old saw about Alaska being like a Dickens novel, George was certainly meeting every character he had even known in this part of the country. Mrs. Burch and her daughter joined us and exchanged excited news about all the people they knew, and I met the whole family. Out of this coffee-drinking, "what's-the-latest-gossip" exchange, I learned that the plane would go to Cordova tomorrow, weather permitting.

I was learning that the whole territory moved to the pace of that phrase: "Weather Permitting."

It was a common joke that I might get a haircut tomorrow, "weather permitting." It turned out to be five days before the "weather permitted" for the plane to Cordova to arrive.

The days began to blur together, just as they had in Whitehorse. Valdez was a little better for me than Whitehorse because at least I had a pleasant friend to spend the time with.

Someone told me that sometimes you could get a ride on a fishing boat if it was going to Cordova. So I asked about the boats in the harbor.

There were two possibilities, a scow and a fishing boat. The scow, it turned out, belonged to friends of George's. We went aboard to inquire and were invited for coffee. I found that you never entered a house or tent or boat in Alaska without being offered coffee. It was the mark of hospitality.

As we sat and talked, we found out the scow wasn't going to Cordova so we signed the guest book and left.

The fishing boat, we learned, was to leave for Cordova at the end of the week, and we could go with them if we were still in Valdez. I must have sloshed down fifteen cups of coffee that first day in the name of hospitality.

On the second day I heard a plane. I had been writing a letter to my mother at the time. I finished the letter rather hastily and dashed down to Burch's. It was the right plane, but headed in the wrong direction; it was bound for Anchorage, not Cordova. Burch said it would try to return to Cordova today—weather permitting.

But the weather didn't permit. Again there were the long, tedious hours sitting in the hotel lobby, listening to the rain on the roof and waiting.

I wrote in my diary: "Perhaps a short description of Valdez would help here. It is built on one street, a considerable extension of which runs clear out into the sea where it joins the boat dock. Because of this long jetty, it might take 15 minutes to see the town in its entirety, walking slowly."

Coming from the dock toward town, George and I joked about the size of it. Looking up the street and reading the signs (exaggerating, of course), we read: "City Limits," "Hotel," "Cafe," "Hospital," "City Limits."

There was no theater, nor any place else to spend the time in the evening other than the bars, and I was too young. So I read magazines, played cribbage and rummy, and read books. I finished 'Scaramouche' by Sabatini while I was weathered in, and it's not a short book.

To relieve the tedium I took a bath and put my hair up in French braids with a big blue ribbon at the back. Then I rummaged through my suitcase for the best clothes I had, a gray, pin-stripe suit and reasonably good shoes (yes, with a penny in them), and went out to join George for dinner. George had never seen me dressed up; jeans and t-shirts were my standard wardrobe. He was suitably impressed and we had a nice dinner at a local restaurant.

On one of these waiting days, I went to the hospital to see whether Nelda O'Laughlen was still there. Nelda was my first roommate in Fairbanks last October, and had been on the bus with me from Whitehorse.

They told me Nelda was Outside at present but might be back on any boat. Also they told me she had been married since starting to work at Valdez. As I said, Alaska abhorred a single woman and married her off as soon as possible. Valdez was especially proud of its record of never letting a single women stay that way.

I needed to get to Cordova!

So I whiled away the time; boredom and "Cabin Fever" was always just around the corner. To make matters worse, George was a better cribbage player than myself! So I made him play rummy instead.

The rain was incessant, a steady drumming on the roof and on the nerves. I was tired of both card games by then, and couldn't find an un-worked crossword puzzle anywhere. After I had devoured the long-winded Sabatini book, I had run out of ideas. So I lay down on the bed in my clothes for a short nap.

Soon there was a knock on the door. I got up to answer it, and found it was the man from across the hall. He invited me to join his group of friends for a drink. The door stood open and nobody seemed to have been drinking much, so out of sheer boredom I joined them in their old-time, Alaska-style gabfest.

The conversation was good, and soon we were joined by others who came and went. It was a nice, lively interval in an otherwise long, tiresome wait.

I was beginning to understand that what Alaskans did for entertainment was to drink gallons of coffee (or gallons of whiskey) and tell stories. The storytelling art was polished by the absence of TV and radio, and I was regaled with tales of hunting incidents, of commercial fishing adventures, of basketball—Alaska lived and breathed basketball—and so on.

The storytelling was full of entertaining anecdotes, punctuated with lots of laughter. I felt good when I left, no longer bored and lonely, and I had lots of things to think about.

Storytelling was the lifeblood of early Alaska, not to be confused with "joke-telling," though we did quite a bit of that too. The storytelling served a purpose. It helped others to avoid the same mistakes that caused the accident/ adventure/ anecdote to happen, and actually was a form of education presented in an entertaining way. You learned how to hunt rabbits, handle guns safely, avoid drowning oneself out fishing, and all sorts of slick little tricks to make life easier. And you got your daily dose of coffee, too.

So it went for five soggy days. On the fifth day the weather was frightful. However, I found out something about Alaskan pilots. If they decide they're going to fly—why, weather be hanged! It suddenly "permits!"

I had just reconciled myself to waiting another day when I heard the plane. Outside the rain poured down with renewed enthusiasm. I threw my things into the suitcase and hurriedly paid the manager. Then, fearful lest Mr. Burch forgot to pick me up, I dashed through the downpour to the store. Valdez's reputation as a marrying place was getting to me!

In Mr. Burch's car we rounded up passengers and baggage. I rushed down to the edge of the bay, where the pilot came wading ashore to give me a piggyback ride in his hip boots out to the plane.

George had his own hip boots with him, being a long-time coastal Alaskan. The pilot was "Mudhole" Smith, and I will always remember that my first meeting with this famous pilot was when he had to carry me on his back out to the plane on my first trip to Cordova.

The trip by air was ridiculously short. I just got used to being up when we circled to land on Eyak Lake in Cordova.

# Chapter Thirteen

## CORDOVA & THE COPPER RIVER FLATS
## June 1946

Eyak Field was a small gravel strip along the edge of Eyak Lake, which lay in a bowl surrounded by mountains. Because of the repair shops located there, Eyak Lake was a fairly important "bush" airfield at that time. (International Airport in Anchorage had not yet been built.) A small dock accommodated floatplanes landing on the lake, so there was no necessity for Smitty to carry us ashore.

Our "float plane" landed on the lake and taxied up to a ramp next to the field. We all climbed into a taxi for the rode to the Windsor Hotel in downtown Cordova. The building must have once been a fine hotel, but now its shabbiness showed through everywhere. Built in 1908, it now looked like the plumbing was all that held the magnificent edifice together.

I decided to try that plumbing by taking a bath. The tub was one of those old jobbies with the eagle-claw feet. One nice thing about Cordova: it had soft water, and I found it a real luxury, especially after the water in Fairbanks.

I sat in the lobby rocking comfortably in a creaky old rocking chair, waiting for George to join me, reflecting on how every hotel lobby in Alaska seemed to have chairs looking out over the town streets.

The Windsor hotel was a local landmark, and its winding, twisting halls gave rise to a lot of jokes about people roaming around in there, lost for years. Built by Michael Heney for his current girlfriend, over the next forty years various additions had been built on without regard to how the hallways would connect. One of its more imaginative managers, in later years, erected highway signs in the halls, with such admonitions as "No U-Turns," "No Parking," and such. The old hotel would last another 35 years after my first stay there, finally succumbing to the ravages of time and the rainy climate.

I thought it was pretty neat, rocking in my chair and watching people go by on the sidewalk outside. Suddenly I looked up to see a cow strolling by, cropping the short grasses that grew alongside the sidewalk.

*Lone E. Janson*

Well, at least Cordova probably has fresh milk, I thought. When George joined me, he told me about Vina Young's herd and her dairy. As we walked along the street, George spoke to old friends by the dozens. It seemed there was no one he didn't know.

He hailed Phyllis Davis, the mayor's wife and an old school chum of George's. She wore an old pair of baggy overalls in which she had been painting their new house.

The three of us together walked to her home to visit. Phyllis fixed George a drink and a beer for me, and went to change. We talked back and forth, and when Phyllis came back, we noticed she was pregnant; in fact she was due in six weeks! I hadn't noticed it when she was in her baggy overalls. She had already been painting for a good eight hours that day.

After a drink and a short visit, we all went down to a little tiny cafe to have spaghetti. We were followed inside by a little cocker spaniel pup called "Murph." Nobody seemed to care, but when I commented on it, Phyllis denied that she owned the pup. Instead, he seemed to be the common property of everyone in town. Phyllis owned the father of the puppy, but the pup had been adopted by almost everyone in town.

Discouraged with us for not feeding him, he moved on to the next table with better success, and stayed with that dinner partner when we left. He was a cute little bum and everyone seemed to love him.

Now we went to a tavern and had an after-dinner drink. It was a short time between fishing seasons, the Copper River season and the upcoming seine season on Prince William Sound. I mentioned trying to find a job and they pointed out where I might go to see about a job in a cannery.

As we visited, somehow we acquired two additions to the party: Bill, a traveling salesman who had been on the same airplane as us, and the mayor Richard Davis. We soon lost Davis, as he suddenly remembered some mayoral item to attend to and was gone, his drink untouched.

Phyllis said, "You see? My child is going to be an orphan!"

George Petersen only stayed a couple of days, and then boarded the plane back to his job on the highway. He left a message in the lobby that he had gone out on the plane. He had to get back to work. I was sorry I didn't have a chance to see him before he left.

By then I was making new friends all around, and even meeting old ones again. I met my old friend from Skagway, Mike Putselas, the Greek who had come up on the Princess Louise last September. I walked into the Model Cafe and there he was. I didn't know him at first, but he knew me.

My mind was fixed on trying to find a job. I had some coffee and went over to the employment service to see about a job. No one was in, so I sat down to wait. As I sat there waiting, it dawned on me who Mike was. Embarrassed to have forgotten, I ran back and exclaimed, "So you're Mike! I'll be darned!" Mike got a good laugh out of that. He treated me with some pastries and coffee there at the old Model Cafe before I returned to the employment office.

There was still no one in the employment office, so I went down to meet the steamer Alaska, just docking. Once again I enjoyed the shouted greetings and exchanges as the steamer came in to the dock and the general air of excitement all around.

Back in the employment office there was finally someone in. Jobs, the man said, were pretty scarce. It was between seasons at the cannery, but he said he might get me on a floating cannery, which would include room and board. He said he'd contact me tomorrow, so I left.

On Main Street I stood leaning on the rail watching the activity in the small boat harbor, and I decided to walk around the docks. Cordova's boat harbor was one of the most picturesque in the world with the men working busily at their boats and gear. "Between seasons" meant a chance to work on balky motors and to mend torn nets.

As I walked the docks, I came upon a fisherman working on his gear, so I paused to watch and exchange a little chitchat. He talked about fishing things, of which I didn't understand very much. Suddenly he handed me a part of the net and said, "Here, hold this taut while I mend this rip." I watched skilled hands mend a tear in the net, the net needle flashing and dodging skillfully between bits of mending twine to become tight knots.

Strolling a little farther I spotted a boat called the Minker. I stopped to ask a question of the two guys who were puttering around on deck. In our conversation I found that the Minker would be a tender for Parks Floater #1, on which I would be working if the employment guy was lucky in getting me the job.

As a tender, the Minker would stand by until the Copper Prince came in from Bering River near Cordova. The owners were two young guys, Martin Stevens ("Steve") and Robert Christen ("Chris"). They invited me to have coffee with them, so I perched on the rail on deck in the bright sunshine, and we talked while we sipped our "Java." By now we were fast friends, and the fact that they would be one of our tenders sealed the friendship.

They told me how they had planned to build the Minker together after the war was over in the South Pacific, and how they had their life savings tied up in her. The name alluded to a desire to raise mink some day.

After a while, exhausted from a full day, I wandered back to the hotel to stretch out for a short nap.

It seems that whenever I lie down fully clothed for a nap, someone knocks on the door. I had nearly dozed off when I heard a knock. It was Bill, our salesman friend. He told me that his brother-in-law Bob Korn, his sister and himself were all going to Bob's hunting lodge on the duck flats and invited me to go.  It was not duck-hunting season, but they were going out to erect a windmill there.

Bob Korn was a very popular local character. He was affectionately called "Kernel Korn," and had a barge by that name. He also owned the Imperial Bar, and was a great supporter of local sports in Cordova, especially basketball. The "Kernel Korn" frequently transported the whole team to games in Valdez.

The hunting lodge on the Copper River Flats sounded like an adventure, so I accepted. He promised to bring me some rubber hip boots and a heavy shirt to use as a jacket. He said to come on down to the dance in about an hour to meet Bob and the others. I was very tired, so I lay down again, fell asleep and completely missed the dance.

About one a.m., the sun still shining brightly down on the Alaskan landscape, Bill was there banging on the door. I climbed into some slacks and overalls (both of them) for warmth. My legs were pretty sensitive where I had frozen them during the winter in Fairbanks.

I opened the door to Bill and he walked in with the promised gear. He plopped the hip boots and heavy shirt down and demanded to know why I hadn't been at the dance. I say demanded but there was no offense in it, for that was simply his way, brusque.

Decked out in hip boots and a heavy shirt about four sizes bigger than I was, I felt completely foolish and could hardly walk down the stairs because of the boots. There I joined those who would be my companions for the next day or so, and we were off in Bob's car with Tony, one of his two golden retrievers, jumping all over us for joy.

Soon we were at Bob's house on Eyak Lake, east of Cordova. There we piled out and the others began donning rubber pants, coats, etc. I was already dressed to the hilt in clumsy water attire, so I spent the time playing with the two dogs, Tony and Chris.

We waded out to Bob's boat and were soon purring smoothly over the quiet waters of Eyak Lake. Bill and I sat on the top while the others occupied the seats. The dogs were neatly stowed under the bow.

There was a channel out across Eyak Lake that was marked with dead trees anchored down. We followed this.

It was not yet 2 a.m. and already broad daylight. Still a cheechako, I got a big kick out of it. After all, this was my first summer in Alaska, and I had never seen the lo-o-ong summer days.

At the far end of the lake we passed under the railroad bridge, part of the abandoned Copper River & Northwestern Railroad, and entered Eyak River. The first part of our passage down Eyak River was through the rain forest, deep green, tangled underbrush, and the summer scent of alders. Surrounded by sheer beauty softened by the light of early morning we sped along, laughing and talking above the roar of the motor. Soon we were out of the trees and onto the duck flats. We burst from the relative gloom and closeness of the rain forest into this wide grassland very suddenly. It spread out as far as the eye could see to the ocean beyond, and behind us the mountains soared. We crossed some sand bars and once came upon a family of ducks. They were swimming along for all they were worth, Mama frightened but refusing to leave the small fry.

This was my first contact with duck flats. Flat is right, for it was perfectly level. I had seen grassy plains in Wyoming, but they were rolling hills, not flat like this. Bill pointed to what looked like three or four tiny boxes off in the distance. "There's where we're going," he announced.

We left the mouth of Eyak River and went far out to sea to avoid the shallow water before turning back toward the little boxes. The channel at the mouth of this slough was narrow and winding, so Bill and Bob debated ways and means of finding it.

We didn't find it; we went aground. Bob revved up the motor and the mud churned up behind us. Bill labored with the one oar and the boat started to move. But not the way we wanted it to. There was no guiding it, so we moved a little and stopped once more, still hard aground. Finally Bill went over the side in his hip boots and pushed. Bob gunned the motor and got out to help Bill. Suddenly the propeller took hold. The boat shot forward and Bill, caught in the wake of it, went swimming. Bob made a mad scramble to get aboard but slipped and joined Bill.

None of us four remaining passengers knew the first thing about piloting a motorboat. Everyone was taken by surprise; I flopped forward and pulled the first knob I could reach. Whether it did any good or not, I don't know, but the boat sure let out a mighty roar as it struck the soft mud of the shore and stopped.

The prop was still making a deafening noise as Bob floundered up laughing so hard he almost choked. I looked back to see Bill, a forlorn and shipwrecked sailor, wading through the shallow water and mud to shore. Everyone was laughing as we climbed onto the shore.

Later, with the boat moored and both of the "swimmers" in dry clothes, we started breakfast. This meal consisted of a box of food imported from town, in spite of Bob's assertion that all one needs to eat well in Alaska is a little salt.

After dishes were cleaned up, we turned in for a little snooze. It had been an early start indeed. The windmill could wait a bit.

After catching up on lost sleep, we all sought out things to do. The men assembled the windmill, with appropriate arguing and cussing, punctuated by the opening of cans of beer.

Some of the women puttered in the kitchen section of the cabin, also opening cans of beer and issuing orders on how to assemble the windmill, orders completely ignored by the men as a matter of course.

Since I had never seen grass flats like this, I went outside to look around, accompanied by the dogs. The bright green duck grass was coarse in texture and was already showing the seed pods that would mature later. The air was thick with mosquitoes, which comprise the main course of dinner to a duck, while we comprise the main course to the mosquito. I was introduced to the mystique of the most popular mosquito repellent of the time: "6-12." The interesting thing about 6-12 is the mosquitoes don't bite, but they land on you and crawl around in the stuff, stopping now and then to massage their tiny feet. It's as if, instead of biting you to death, they are determined to tickle you to death.

Bob Korn's cabin had an outhouse, of course. I made use of it and found it quite interesting. Since we were surrounded by miles and miles of miles and miles, the outhouse door simply faced away from the cabin and needed no physical door at all. Bob was fond of saying that his was the only outhouse in Alaska "where you can take care of business and shoot a duck at the same time."

Along about afternoon, the windmill was assembled and the beer was getting low, so we started to make "going home" noises and motions. Back in the skiff, the sun still blazing merrily away in the sky, we headed back out through the tortuous channel (having considerably better luck getting out than coming in), and up Eyak River to the lake. It had been a tremendously interesting day to me.

The next day I showed up at the employment office to find that I had a job on the floating cannery. I was to report right away to Parks Floater #1, moored down by the Ocean Dock near the canneries.

# Chapter Fourteen

## PARKS FLOATER #1

### July 1946

Once more I took my "bindle" and headed for the cannery dock where the two scows comprising Parks Floater #1 were tied up. There was a cannery scow and a warehouse scow, and the living quarters were in the upper part of the cannery scow. The Minker was tied up alongside, and Steve especially seemed happy to see that I had gotten the job.

I met the superintendent, George Prater, who said that I could move in right away, so I went into the deserted women's dorm and took possession of an upper bunk with a window. It was a happy choice, for at Esther Island I had the view of the waterfall through that window all summer.

Mr. Prater sent me over to the shore-side cannery to work a bit while we were in port. My first job was cutting out halibut cheeks. I didn't know halibut had cheeks, and I certainly didn't know halibut were so BIG. We had one halibut that must have topped 300 lbs, because it completely covered the huge table we had and hung over the side. I cut out the cheeks on this giant and weighed them—they weighed in at 1 3/4 pounds each!

George Prater's wife and daughter, both named Anne, and his son Georgie, soon joined us aboard the floater. They had separate quarters so we didn't see much of them till we got to the island. There were several people who were full-time employees (as opposed to summer cannery workers like myself). They took care of the machinery and the can line. There was Bell, the mechanic; and Pappy, whose bailiwick seemed to be boilers; and one couple, Dave and June Conkey. The Conkeys were delightful people. June was short, brown, and bubbly like a stubby of beer. Dave was fairly quiet and a little on the intellectual side. The two of them got along well all the time and provided entertaining conversation and companionship. They were well educated, and this added to their charm.

One day Dave started quoting poetry to me beginning with a passage from "Thanatopsis" and ranging through many of my brother's favorites from his college days. I recognized many of them and would call out the names as he recited. It was unplanned, fun and challenging. I thought I didn't do too well. I know my brother would have scoffed because I couldn't remember some of the authors, but Dave was flabbergasted. "She knows them all!" he declared. He had never been around my brother; he would have out-quoted Dave and maybe even stumped him once or twice.

After a couple of days, a few of the crew started checking in and staking claims to bunks in the women's dorm. There was Lil Beyers, who was born and raised not only in Alaska but in Prince William Sound, and Carolyn, redheaded and delightfully crazy. She was close to my own age and we became good friends even though she right away moved in on Steve, who was on the verge of becoming my steady beau. I think Carolyn was a little disappointed when she couldn't get a rise out of me over Steve, but the fact was that I didn't want to get too serious over anyone yet. I still had a lot of Alaska to see. Besides, there was this nagging feeling that if a fellow was that easy to lose, well, so be it, and we all remained friends.

After the halibut cheeks, while we were still in port, they put me to work feeding can lids to the machines. Even though I found the clash and noise of the cannery rather exciting, I have to admit that of all the jobs I have ever held, feeding lids has to be the most boring and stupid. I just stood there with an open box of lids alongside of me, and whenever the stack got down low enough I put some more lids in, trying not to fall asleep in the meantime.

But I had a chance to try out my new cannery boots and rain gear for the job, and to put on the long rubber aprons and clean cannery gloves we were issued every day.

I learned lots of new phrases like "Iron Chink," so called because this fish-cleaning machine replaced the Chinese crews that used to do that work by hand. From where I fed the lids, I could see the filler girls fitting the fish together to go into the machine, and the "patch table" where the girls weighed cans that looked too heavy or too light, and snipped off any stray bones or fins that poked up out of the cans. I learned that there was "wet" and "dry" work, and that feeding lids was classed as "wet" work, so was paid maybe a nickel more an hour than the "dry" work in the can loft or warehouse. I always felt there should have been another bonus for sheer boredom.

We had coffee breaks every two hours, and the rolls, cakes and other goodies spread out at coffee breaks were fabulous. They really fed us good in the canneries. I ate at the mess hall on shore during this interval in town. It was between seasons, so there weren't many fish, the hours were short, and the weather was sunny and warm.

One day while we were sitting on the deck of the warehouse killing time, we decided to make ice cream. George Prater produced an old-fashioned ice cream churn, and Dave Conkey appeared with buckets of ice and a big bag of rock salt. June provided the recipe and mixed it using "armored cow" (canned milk) in the recipe, and the result was great. I was first to sit on the maker while Lil cranked, then we traded off on the cranking, now and then opening the case up to add ice and salt. While she was not cranking, Carolyn produced a guitar and strummed a few tunes. We sat around talking and listening to soft music as we ate ice cream and soaked up the warm June sunshine there on the Cordova dock.

*Carolyn playing guitar. Lone sits on the left.*

*Lone E. Janson*

*Lil Beyers making ice cream as crew watches.*

The next day, Friday, the Copper Queen arrived early in the morning from Bering River and made ready to take one of the scows in tow. The rest of the crew arrived and took up residence in the women's dorm or elsewhere. The cannery was coming to life.

It would take several big tenders to tow the two fully loaded scows to Esther Island, plus one or two for stand-by and emergencies. I think they were possibly the Redondo or the Redhead or both. I don't think the Copper King put in a showing for another week or so, probably still cleaning up the Bering River operation. There was one smaller tender that accompanied the flotilla, the Copper Prince. We got a big kick out of the "Copper family" of tenders.

The smaller tenders, like the Minker, left for the island to get things ready, like attaching cables to shore, rigging water lines, and such preparations for our arrival. We were all ready to go, or so I thought, when things came to a halt. I was excited and antsy, itching to get under way. "What's the big hold-up?" I asked. Mr. Prater just chuckled tolerantly and said: "Well, it's Friday, and one of our skippers refuses to begin any voyage on a Friday. Old sailor's superstition, you know." So we waited overnight and left on next morning's tide.

What a beautiful Saturday it was. Bright and sunny, but I didn't know at that time that bright, sunny days on Prince William Sound frequently bring on a Westerly slop in the afternoon. Such a sea can be quite unsettling, with the sun, the sea, and your stomach all dancing around.

We enjoyed the first part of the voyage as we were towed between beautiful green wooded islands past scenes of unequalled splendor. It was like the Inside Passage all over again: the deep, mysterious fiords, the bright sparkling green water, the dense forests, seaweed a golden hue along the shores, and teeming with sea life. Here and there a seal would break the surface, ducks and sea birds were everywhere, a sea lion lazed on a buoy, and now and then a salmon made his spectacular leap. Off in the distance the tall dorsal of a killer whale made its appearance, followed by his flukes as he dove. A pod of porpoises frolicked around our bow then shot off like a streak after faster games to play.

We ate cold sandwiches for lunch because we had no electricity during the tow to the island. Coffee could be obtained on the Copper Prince alongside.

*Lone E. Janson*

After lunch we passed Knowles Head and entered a stretch of water that was open to a swell from Hinchinbrook Entrance. The ride began to be uncomfortable as the towlines tended to slack off then snap taut with a jerk. So the tender eased back and tied up alongside, towing from there. Despite the numerous bumpers and fenders between the scows and the tenders, the ride was becoming distinctly unpleasant as the fair-weather Westerly began to pick up. One by one passengers began to ease out of the dining room. Carolyn and I peeked into the dorm and found a number of unhappy forms sprawled on bunks with buckets conveniently near. One of the sufferers raised her head in a wobbly fashion and declared solemnly, "I don't feel good when I'm sick!" and her head plopped back down on the pillow. Carolyn and I found this solemn declaration very funny, but we tried to hold our laughter till we were out of ear-shot.

I decided the best thing was to stay on deck if possible. That helped for a while, but the horizon refused to remain still, and try as I might, my balance mechanism started to act up. I have to admit that it wasn't too much longer before I joined my suffering shipmates in the women's dorm. I was distinctly, undeniably seasick, and our sufferer had been right, I didn't feel good when I was sick, either.

*Ladies on the floater. Lone bottom left (sitting).*

*Lone E. Janson*

With the slop, the tenders had to ease off on their speed, and the tow to Esther Island had taken all night (which of course did not get dark at all). I woke the next morning feeling fine but a little wobbly. The decks were steady, though I could tell we were still under tow. But looking out my view window, I could see we were within a protected bay. I jumped up and ran out to see what Esther Island looked like.

What a marvelous place! It was green and wooded, with mountains all around. The water was deep blue in the center, deep green around the edges, and so clear you could see the salmon swimming away from the boat. At the head of the bay was a small spawning stream, but when we rounded a point we beheld the most beautiful sight of all. A lovely cascade of water roared down from the mountain above. The waterfall dominated the little bight where we were securing the warehouse and cannery by strong cables to the shore. This would be my home for the next month or so.

Over the next couple of days, with a good chart from one of the boats, I learned a few more details of this grand setting where I was to live my summer. At the top of the falls, there was a huge lake, Esther Lake, some ten miles or more long, and possibly a mile wide. It was a

*Parks Floating Cannery.*

*Lone E. Janson*

tremendously deep lake. This lake fed the cataract that tumbled down to a small quiet pond halfway down the mountain where Dolly Varden trout teemed. From this pond, the cascade began again in roaring splendor, and this was the part of the falls I beheld daily from my "picture window" as I lay on the upper bunk in the women's dorm.

I had the big chart spread out on the dining room table and several of us were looking it over. We planned some picnics up to the lake, and looked over the nearby bays we hoped to explore as time allowed. We traced the many islands of Prince William Sound, discussing what we thought the season would be like.

I looked up, laughing. The rest of the crew wanted to know what was so funny.

"I think I've found my home!" I declared. "There's an island for each one of my names, including my middle one. There's a Lone Island, an Esther Island, and a Green Island. That's my name: Lone Esther Green!"

Happily, I went back to the dorm and dug out a swimming suit. It was a warm day, and the water looked fine. I ran out on deck and dived overboard. The water was warm (or at least, not particularly cold). I would find out in later years that if the water is clear, it has a good

*The "6:30 Club"*

chance of being warm, but if it's cloudy or milky, there's a good chance it's extremely cold because glacier water is always milky.

The water on Esther Island, especially in this protected bight, was so nice and warm that I was quickly joined by two of the guys, and we began the practice of getting up at 6:30 a.m. to take a dip before breakfast and work. We became known as the "6:30 Club." We swam almost every morning that summer, and the water was wonderful. The only drawback was the jellyfish that abounded throughout the Sound, and stung if you brushed against them.

The fishermen from the boats watched this performance with some awe. I was to find that most resident Alaskan fishermen could not swim, although they spent their lives on the water. Thinking on it, this was not so surprising. Swimming is a vigorous activity; learning to swim is not. Someone like me, who had access to warm indoor pools and equally warm waters outside at an early age, learned as a matter of course. Once learned, vigorous activity in much colder waters quickly warmed one up and there is no problem, but to learn in such cold water is prohibitive. There was not one indoor pool in the entire territory at that time, and as a consequence many fishermen drowned under circumstances that need not have led to their deaths.

*Untangling line from prop.*

My swimming skills were called into service within the first week or so, on a day when the Minker was to head for Cordova. This small tender and Copper Prince were sent to town frequently for supplies of various kinds. But on this day, they had somehow gotten the propeller caught in 4-strand seine rope. They weren't sure how badly the rope was tangled and asked if I would dive under the boat and find out if it was just around the prop or wound around the shaft, too. It seems that propeller shafts are made of Monel metal, something slightly more valuable than pure gold, and that 4-strand nylon seine rope can cut one in two if the shaft is turned while a rope is around it.

I was delighted. Feeling enormously important, I dived down underneath the boat, something I had never done till then. I remember the weird feeling of swimming up under the stern, grabbing the rudder and hand-over-handing to the prop blade and the shaft, where I found the rope thoroughly and tightly wound. The water was murky green and shadowy down there. I could see a little but not much, but the fact that the rope was there was undeniable.

When I popped up to the surface and gave my report, my importance ended. Chris jumped overboard, clothes and all, to begin cutting it loose, aided by Johnny, a strapping young Native aboard the floater. Under no circumstances would they let me help cut it loose, so I threw Johnny's coat over my shoulders and stood by on Johnny's skiff in case they changed their minds. Carolyn manned the skiff, and Molly, another Native girl, held a rope over the stern for the boys to hang on to when resting between dives. They had to hold their breath during dives, cut awhile, come up for air, then go down again.

Eventually they cut it loose, and the shaft was okay. I learned a few inner secrets of boats, about Monel metal shafts, and the incredible cutting quality of nylon ropes. Also, it was fun to feel that my swimming abilities were needed on occasion.

*Dora Hansen and Lone*

# Chapter Fifteen

## ESTHER ISLAND—FIRST YEAR
### Summer 1946

By the end of the first week, I was becoming familiar with the cannery and how salmon were canned. First the fishing boat would pull up alongside and the fishermen would begin pitching the salmon with a "peugh" (pronounced "pew") onto the fish elevator. I never tired of watching the elevator bring up its gleaming load of salmon. The fish elevator had a series of ladder-like steps on a conveyer belt. It was like a fish escalator. From there another belt carried the salmon to the bins where they'd go through the "Iron Chink," the machine that took out the insides, guts and gurry.

From the Iron Chink the fish passed on a belt to the sliming table, where the slimers removed any remaining fins or blood next to the backbone, and in general cleaned the fish up before sending it off to the filler bin, where I worked. We would open a hatchway on the bottom of the fish bin to allow fish to slide down to the filler, where we arranged them so that the machine would cut the fish to fit into the cans.

It was fast work and generally kept us busy enough that I was not bored—it sure beat feeding lids to the machine. I worked occasionally on the patch table and got pretty good at grabbing cans which were too heavy or too light. We used a scissors to snip off a piece from heavy ones, and for the light ones, we added small patches brought to us by the Filipino crews. A quick snip was enough to take care of stray bones or fins. The resultant pack was beautiful to see and scrumptious to eat.

All the cleanings (or "fish gurry") that came off the Iron Chink and the sliming tables was dumped in the water, where small Dolly Varden trout gathered for the feast.

Since the floater had only the small 7-oz. cans, the machinery was rather slow and we filler girls often got ahead of the can line. When this happened, we'd stop feeding the line and go out on a little side balcony nearby. Here we'd kneel down and begin catching small fish with our bare hands. It took quiet waiting and a quick grab. It was lots of fun to catch a small pile of them that way, and we competed to see who could catch the most before getting back to work on the filler.

The floater had many new experiences for me. Living with the tide was one. Tides are rather large in Prince William Sound, and getting to feel the rhythm of its rise and fall, its gradual daily time change and all, I found fascinating. And of course the fishermen lived by those tides. I also learned how to tell if a tender had many fish aboard as it came around the point. You could tell by how deep in the water she was riding.

One time all the machinery unexpectedly came to a stop. I was looking around to discover what mysterious reason there could be for this. Some of the workers were leaving their posts on the can line and heading out to the warehouse scow. I followed them out there and found the whole crew gathered by the big sliding doors overlooking the beach near the waterfall.

"What's going on?" I asked.

With a motion to be very quiet, one of the workers pointed to shore where a mink sat poised and waiting. Suddenly without rippling a muscle, he splashed into the water and came up with a fish in his mouth. He ignored our presence. He darted into the woods, and in exactly three minutes was back, ready to catch another fish. He must

*Ben Durkee*

have been feeding a family, because he never ate any of the fish. His pattern was invariable and precisely timed and very efficient. He'd watch, spring, catch the fish and dart into the woods, and reappear again. We must have watched him fish for an hour, and only once did I see him miss a fish.

We didn't have a name for the bay in which the floater was anchored, so after that, we dubbed the bay "Mink Bay." It was later named Lake Bay.

Saturday and Sunday were closed fishing seasons, so we canned Friday's catch on Saturday, and by afternoon we usually were done. The whole crew adjourned to the warehouse where we all cased up what salmon cans were cool, so we'd have room to hold a dance that evening.

We either danced to phonograph music or perched on the coolers of canned salmon listening to the music and visiting. The dances in the floater warehouse were always enjoyable and of course there were plenty of schottisches and polkas.

We'd dance and visit with the fishermen, occasionally go aboard the boats where there was always a pilothouse gabfest going on. The fishermen exchanged stories of their adventures and misadventures, and

*Taking a break among the cans on the Floater.*

told tall stories full of lies calculated to keep the others from knowing where the best fishing spots were.

Most of the stories were about "crik robbing," and how to avoid the "fish bugs" who stood by to arrest them if they got caught. I was shocked at this blatant disregard for the law. I protested, "But that's against the law! You rob creeks of their fish?"

"Hey, this is nothing to the robbery going on by the Alaska Salmon Industry! They're looting the whole Territory and putting nothing back, and we have not one thing to say about it. I don't know about you, but I think if it's okay for the salmon canners to 'Get in, Get Yours, and Get out!' then I'm going to do the same thing!"

They told me how all fishing regulations for the coming season were made in Washington, D.C., the winter before, after consulting with the major canning company lobbyists as to what they wanted. The Washington bureaucrats had no idea of Alaska fisheries and were easy prey for the Alaska Salmon Industry, Inc., which kept a flotilla of lobbyists on hand in the capital.

An angry fisherman explained to me: "In the Russian days they used to say 'Heaven is high, and the Czar is far away!' so they got away with anything. Now it's 'Heaven is high, and Washington is far away!' It's always the same! The canning interests are running Alaska!" "Yeah," came another voice, "Running it right into the ground!"

Grunts and nods of agreement, and another angry voice: "We won't get control of our fisheries till we get Statehood, and we won't get Statehood till there's not another fish in the streams for the canning interests to scrape out, so let's get with the program!"

It was my baptism by fire into the "scorched earth" policy that the rank and file of Alaska fishermen had unofficially and almost unanimously adopted. Alaskan fishermen were waging a silent, effective war. There were many facets to this "war" that I would learn as time went by.

Meanwhile, we on the floater were dedicated to enjoying the summer. Young fishermen came aboard the floater on weekends with their soap and towels to get a nice hot shower and to flirt with the young girls on the can lines. I was having a ball, swimming, riding around in skiffs, and enjoying myself. Because of my "6:30 Club" activities, everyone knew I loved to swim and one day one of the fishermen pushed me overboard. This was something I would have found fun and hilarious,

*Swimming in Esther Lake.*

except that I had my glasses on, and they ripped off my face and went to Davy Jones' locker. I was effectively blind till I could get a new pair sent out from town. Prater ordered them the same day by radio, but it would be several weeks before "Mudhole Smith," the pilot, could bring them out. "Mudhole" ran Cordova Airlines, which flew out weekly to all the canneries with mail.

Since I couldn't really see well, Mr. Prater put me to work stitching boxes in the warehouse. The boxes came in flattened piles, and were stitched with metal staples. It took a little practice to handle the stitcher, but after a while I got so I could place six staples just perfectly in the bottom of the box, give it a swift whirl with a flourish and get the next six stitches in without blinking an eye. It was fun—almost dramatic if the flourish was any good.

On weekends the fishermen watched this performance and begged me to let them try the machines. Soon all I had to do was sit on the soft piles of boxes and egg them on, telling stories and enjoying myself, while the fishermen stitched the boxes for me. It was Tom Sawyer with a new twist!

The three Hansen girls, Mae, Dora, and Louise, became my particular buddies on the floater that year. They were called the "Mad Hansens," and we had lots of fun together, especially on trips to town.

*Lone E. Janson*

*Louise Hansen with Bill Rice, Dick Fitzgibbons, and Charlie Liljegren at Esther Island.*

The Hansen girls were part of a large family from Katalla, which was by then a ghost town. Several of their brothers fished for Parks Floater. One Saturday Roy Hansen took me out on the bay in his skiff, and there I got to know the differences between the five species of salmon. There were Kings, Reds, Pinks, Dogs, and Silvers. Each of the five had another name: Reds were also Sockeyes and Pinks were also called Humpbacks or "Humpies." Kings were Chinooks. It was too early in the year for many silvers, and the majority of our fish were Humpies and Dogs (Chum salmon). The reds brought the best price on the shelf. Their texture was excellent, and the color was pleasing to the eye.

As we rowed around out there on Mink Bay, Roy pointed out how the different species could be recognized just by the way they jumped out of the water. Humpies were a dead giveaway; they flipped up in a sort of athletic curl and plopped back. Flip, plop! Reds were a much bigger fish and leaped more or less high and straight, re-entering the water with little disturbance, rarely falling on the flat side. Silvers were

*Lone standing on a fish trap.*

*Lone E. Janson*

bright, graceful and streamlined, but frequently deliberately hit the water on their sides with a loud smack, as if to loosen the eggs inside. And so on, till I could tell what kind of salmon just by the way it leaped out of the water.

In the cannery itself I learned to identify them by their own particular look or markings. King salmon had small black spots on their backs, and Humpies (Pinks) had large black spots. Dolly Varden trout had pink spots and we were instructed to toss them out when they came along. We ignored this, called them "pink-spotted Kings" and canned them with the Humpies. We considered this a great joke. It was harmless, because Dollies are good eating anyway.

King salmon were the best tasting, but because of their color, canned Red salmon brought the best price. In the early days of canneries, only Reds were canned. Red salmon were called "Redfish" back then. Later they began to can the pink-fleshed Humpies, and to enhance the appeal of the paler pinks, one canner put on his label: "Guaranteed not to turn red in the can"!

Roy was full of the fundamental lore of Alaska and its fisheries, having virtually grown up on a fishing boat, and I enjoyed these outings.

I went on a number of boat trips that summer. One weekend I was able to go with one of the tenders, the Redhead, on a trip to the cannery on Evans Island. It was a short trip, but it was then that I learned to steer a boat, both visually and by compass bearing. I really enjoyed that, and on the return trip I did almost all the steering, matching visual sightings and blinking buoy lights to those shown on the charts. I took great pleasure in this new skill.

The season was getting ready to close. Fishing had been extremely poor, and we had been working an average of an hour or less a day on the can line. The rest of the day we just goofed off. We were looking forward to the end of the season.

But then came the real shocker: the season was extended two more weeks! The lobbyists in D.C. had convinced the Fish & Wildlife people that the run was late, and that "millions of pinks were rounding Hinchinbrook Entrance into the Sound." We all knew this was garbage, but how could they know it in Washington, D.C.? Heaven was indeed high, and Washington indeed far away.

The isolation and lack of work was getting to us. George Prater especially felt the strain of trying to keep a young and boisterous crew from going off the deep end one way or another.

He decided we needed a day in town, so he and most of our crew headed for Cordova on the Copper Prince. We were all in need of some rest and recreation ("R&R"), having been out on Esther Island over five weeks by then. We called it being "bush happy." The prospect of two more weeks was overwhelming. It was good to see the lights of a real, honest-to-goodness town again, even one as small as Cordova.

We were like caged animals turned loose. Teamed up with the "Mad Hansens," I made the circuit of all the bars. We were letting off steam, laughing and thinking up deviltry to get into. Bob Korn's Imperial Bar was really busy, full of fishermen in town for the weekend closure. Dora, one of the Mad Hansens, came over and whispered to us: "Let's empty this bar out and take everyone over across the street to the Little Bar!" I looked over to where the Little Bar didn't have a single patron.

"Great idea!" I said, "Let's do it!"

It was incredibly easy, just a pass along the bar by all four of us, urging the fishermen, "Come on, we're going over to the Little Bar!" In five minutes flat, the Imperial was totally empty and the Little Bar was totally full of laughing, uproarious fishermen and, of course, the "Mad Hansens" and myself. We looked over and the bartender at the Imperial was taking off his apron, locking up that bar for a while, and coming over to join us! It was a real power trip to see what four young girls could do to a whole bar full of young men.

We decided that was so much fun, we'd try to get ourselves arrested. Actually we didn't have a Chinaman's Chance of that. In the wild and wooly atmosphere of Old Cordova during the fishing season, there was no way we could raise enough Hell to ruffle the feathers of the night cop, if there was even one on duty. But it was a nice fantasy.

Prater knew what he was doing. He had warned us we were leaving on the evening tide, so before long he had us rounded up and aboard the Copper Prince again. The entire crew of that small tender was drunk, or at least tipsy. Prater had had a few drinks, but I had the feeling he was neither tipsy nor drunk, though he joined in the banter and general spirit of the occasion. He was probably just happy to have gotten his whole crew back on the Copper Prince in time for the return to Esther

*Lone E. Janson*

Island, without even one worker "jumping ship" or quitting. He must have sighed with relief when we slipped the ropes and left the dock.

I was feeling high-spirited too. I remembered a silly limerick I had once heard and recited it to the tipsy crew:

> *"A canner exceedingly canny*
> *Once remarked to his granny:*
> *'A canner can can*
> *Anything that he can,*
> *But a canner can't can a can, can he?'"*

It is indicative of the alcoholic lubrication of the crew that they thought this hilarious. Prater had one of his own. Like a Roman Senator he struck a pose and intoned gravely: "We are not Vast Cannerymen. We are Half-Vast Cannerymen!"

This witticism was hailed with gales of laughter. I looked up, and there outside the pilothouse window loomed a solid rock wall right ahead of us! I grabbed the wheel and put it hard over to miss bumping into a cliff. After that, I figured I'd better keep an eye on whoever (if anyone) was steering.

The skipper sent one of the crew to the wheel topside. Prater stood in the pilothouse next to an open window, passing the whiskey bottle from the pilothouse helmsman to the other crewmembers and back again.

As we got farther from town, gradually members of the cannery crew began to bunk down wherever they could. Several of them slept under the galley table, and I guess one or two on top. The bunks were all full and there were snoring bodies wrapped in sleeping bags all over the deck. The skipper was at the helm and darkness had fallen. We had reached Knowles Head and could see far ahead the vague outline of Storey, Peak, and Naked islands. It was obvious that the skipper was very tired, so I offered to stand wheel watch for a while. He was happy to surrender the wheel to me. He pointed out the blinking light off the point of Storey Island to steer for, and said to wake him when I came abeam of it, and he'd give me a new heading. Then he hit the sack in the fo'csle.

Suddenly the world was quiet, and I was alone at the wheel. Our wake glowed with phosphorus. Ahead the moon gleamed on the dark water, and faint navigation lights blinked their friendly beacons to me. The stars sparkled overhead, undimmed by any light except the soft green glow of the compass. How beautiful was the world! I steered for several hours toward Storey Island light, enjoying every moment of it. I looked again at the phosphorus gleaming in the wake of the boat, sighing with pleasure.

But at last I had to awaken the skipper for a new heading. For a while I steered while he pointed out bearings and made us some hot black coffee. Later, I sipped coffee while he steered, and finally I joined the mummy-like forms on the deck for a few hours of sleep.

I woke a little later when the boat slowed down, and got up to see the most beautiful sight of all. It was still dark as we rounded the point into Mink Bay, and there we beheld the floater itself, decked out in bright lights that shimmered across the dark water toward me. The tumbling cascade behind the floater glowed a dimmer white, and the mountains loomed black and mysterious against a starlit sky. Surely, this was the wonderful adventure I sought in Alaska. I was supremely happy, in spite of the extra two weeks of isolation we had to endure.

As we expected, the "millions of salmon" turned out to be the same sorry dibble of fish, and then, to our intense amazement and disgust, the pundits in Washington granted us ANOTHER week! "What for?" I asked the fishermen, "So we can scrape every fish available out of the water?"

The fishermen shook their heads at me. "You don't think like a cannery operator. In their business, they must meet a quota to fill their orders for canned salmon. But if there are too many fish, their inventory will be too high and the price will drop too low. So when the fishing is good, they tell the Fish & Wildlife that fishing is lousy, and get an early closure. But when fishing is bad, they haven't filled their quotas, so they want extensions."

My mind was whirling. "But that's just the opposite of what constitutes good fisheries management!"

The fishermen nodded. "Now you're getting the picture," they said.

A couple of days before we went back to town, the Copper Prince was dispatched out to the head of the bay to make soundings to see if there was enough depth for the Alaska Steamship to anchor and take

*Lone E. Janson*

*Taking the fish from a fish trap. Fish traps were thought to be largely responsible for depleting the fisheries.*

on our canned fish. I went along and really enjoyed the process of making the soundings. We ran out of line at 37 fathoms. That meant that we had plenty of depth but probably no holding bottom, since the depth right here, less than a mile from shore was about 250 feet. On the way back to the floater we had an escort of porpoises, the sailor's best omen. It was Thursday then; we were to be towed back to town on Saturday, August 31.

The familiar commotion and general battening-down of cargo and loose objects was almost "old hat" to me by now. In preparation for getting under way again, the Copper King, Queen, and Prince all scuttled around, their crews helping untie ropes, unhitch water lines and performing other rites of separation. I gathered that it was not feasible for the steamer to pick up our fish, because the crews spent some time securing the canned salmon in the warehouse scow. Soon it was Saturday, and the two scows were rounding the point of what we called "Mink Bay," riding at the end of long tow lines.

Carolyn and I leaned on the rail of the Copper Queen watching it all and talking.

I told her, "Tomorrow is the anniversary of my arrival in Alaska. I landed in Alaska a year ago tomorrow. And I've been here for one full winter. Tomorrow I'll be a Sourdough! A year ago I'd never been on a boat in my life. My voyage to Skagway was my first, and here I am, taking another water voyage. Life's funny, isn't it?"

"Yeah," chuckled Carolyn, then asked, "What do you want to do after the season?"

"I've been thinking that the one place I really want to see is Nome. You know, the Gold Rush and all that. I'd like to see Nome."

"I'm going to stay aboard and work the Dungeness crab season out at Anderson Bay. Why don't you stay with the floater? There should be three weeks, maybe a month more of work out there."

I thought it over a while, but the season was getting late and I wanted to see Nome before freeze-up. Nome appealed to me, probably because it was so offbeat, but mostly I was restless, tired of the floater, and I wanted to see more of Alaska. "No," I said, "If I'm going to winter in Nome I need to get settled. I'd better go now."

"Hmm. Nome. I've never had any wish to go there. How do you get to Nome?" asked Carolyn.

"I've looked into it," I assured her. "You catch the boat to Seward, then the Alaska Railroad to Fairbanks, and I guess from there you can find a plane of some kind."

"Well, the next boat west comes in day after tomorrow. The Baranof will be in late that day; I know because Steve's dad is coming in."

"Steve's dad is coming in? Gee, that'll be nice for you and Steve to visit with him. Maybe I'll have a couple of hours to meet him while the freight is unloaded."

The voyage to town was long and tedious. No one even got seasick. There was nothing much to do during that long weary time except play cards, drink coffee, and talk. We hit the sack early.

The next morning found us just around the point from Cordova. As soon as we docked, I went uptown to check my mail and look for some new shoes; the ones I was still wearing had a flapping sole and there wasn't a thing I could do about it. There was no mail for me, of course, because the boat wasn't due till day after tomorrow, as Carolyn said. The shoe store was closed because it was Sunday. I only hoped I didn't have to wait for the boat to dock for the store to have the right size in stock again, because then I wouldn't have time to get a new pair. I borrowed a pair of shoes for the dance that evening. They didn't fit well, but I mostly danced in my sock feet anyway.

I enjoyed being in town again. We ran into the crew from the Copper Prince and the Redondo in the Alaskan bar, where there was dancing every weekend, especially at season-end. It was my first contact with Cordova during the after-season celebration. Everyone had worked hard out fishing; they had collected their paychecks—in some cases all they would make that year, or at least the lion's share of it. It was natural and traditional that everyone would go out and celebrate a bit. Most folks paid their past winter's bills and then used the rest for a gigantic blowout party. It was a good old Sourdough custom, dating back to gold rush days, part of the Sourdough credit system.

For the next two days, we partied. We bar-hopped from Bob Korn's Imperial Bar to the Club to the Little Bar and the Cordova House, and finally we danced in the Alaskan Bar to the music of Peggy French and Bertha Glud, piano and accordion, and there were lots of schottisches and polkas that really got the circulation up. Friends and acquaintances from the fishing fleet and the floater came and went, and we all had a wonderful time dancing till early morning. When at last the Alaskan closed, we all adjourned to Don McCollum's apartment. Nobody was home, but Don had invited us, and the door was unlocked according to custom, so we went right in and made a pot of coffee and visited. I don't remember if Don was with us or not. We danced some more to the phonograph.

Presently Don's mother came in and stood uncertainly in the doorway, weaving just a trifle. She was feeling no pain, and didn't seem a bit non-plussed over the party going on in her living room. In a loud, disgusted voice she announced, "I broke my hat!"

We looked at each other, wondering how she could break her hat. Was it made of wood or glass or something? Before we could ask her, she turned around and left. The party went on.

It was very late—or rather, very early—when we got back to the darkened floater. We turned in for a long sleep before getting up the next day to move all our gear out and find a place to stay. I didn't need a place. I was catching the steamship Baranof that night, bound for Seward. But I did manage to get a new pair of shoes, "penny loafers" with a slot in the top where I could tuck my penny. Now I would be much more comfortable for the upcoming trip to Nome.

# Chapter Sixteen

## AFTER THE SEASON'S OVER
### September 1946

In post-war years, it was actually easier to go to Seattle from Cordova than to go anyplace in Alaska. A voyage in either direction required a long wait for an Alaska Steamship boat, but going south was easier. It required only boarding the boat and sailing five days to Seattle. Northbound, however, entailed landing in either Valdez or Seward and then finding other transportation to go northward. From Valdez there was a road; from Seward only the Alaska Railroad connected with the interior. There were no roads from Seward to the Kenai Peninsula or elsewhere as yet. In either case, there was a wait of from a day to a week to get on your way again.

There were few airlines in the wake of World War II. The War had taken all the planes from civilian service, and new routes were still in the process of developing. Air travel was fraught with "mechanicals." I didn't mind the "mechanicals" on the ground; it was the "mechanicals" in the air that undid my mental equilibrium.

I would encounter a rich variety of all these things on my trip to Nome, which took four or five days. Alaska Steam called in Cordova every ten days northbound, and two days later southbound. Sailing to Seward required one day. From there it was two LONG days on the Alaska Railroad to Fairbanks, and another day or two to find an airplane to fly to Nome. The flight to Nome was six or seven hours.

Back then just getting in or out of road-less Cordova was the problem. Even though the right-of-way of the Copper River & Northwestern Railway had been given free of charge to the government with the proviso that it be "for a public highway," there was no money for road construction for reasons I learned on the bus trip over the Richardson Highway. Ever philosophical, people in Cordova jokingly said, "Nobody will come into Cordova, but the entire population will probably drive out!" This remark was usually accompanied by lots of laughter and another round of drinks. In those days, we were still sure we'd have it eventually. Cordova had always been a transportation hub;

nobody doubted it was still such. The railroad had only been closed six years, including a world war, which stopped everything.

I was fortunate in having to wait only two days for the Baranof on its northbound voyage; otherwise the after-fishing partying might have done me in.

Carolyn, Butch, and the "Mad Hansens" came with me down to the dock to watch the boat come in; everyone did that anyway. It was dark, after midnight, and the Baranof was ablaze with lights. She looked like a glittering ballet dancer as she slid ever closer to the crowded pier. As soon as we could make out faces, we were waving to old friends, and shouting our hellos across the diminishing distance. Among ourselves, we were already remarking who was back, and who was with new wives or babies, long before the boat was moored and the gangplank in place. When Steve's dad came down the gangplank, we knew him instantly because he looked just like his son. We joined the general exodus to the post office to await the arrival of our mail, and sure enough, there was a letter from my mother. How good it was to hear from her! I was glad I had already mailed my letter to her, so it would go out on this boat's southbound leg. We had about four hours while the boat was longshored. Some of the fishermen joined the crews for that operation and supplemented their income during the winter by doing longshore work.

The floater crew saw another chance to try to talk me into staying for the crab season. We went to someone's house for coffee and they urged me to join them at Anderson Bay. "It will be lots of fun, and we can make some more money before winter!" I declined again. By now my mind was made up and I was primed to go to Nome. Getting there before winter seemed paramount, and I suspected winter came early to Nome.

So a few hours later I found myself on the Baranof waving goodbye to friends who shouted: "Bon Voyage! Have a nice trip!" from the receding dock. There they were, at this heathenishly early hour, seeing me off. Carolyn, Butch, Steve, Steve's dad, the "Mad Hansens," Roy Hansen, and many of their relatives, the Praters, and the rest of the crew, too, all there to see me off. At that moment how I hated to leave! But the booming whistle reverberated from the mountains, the lines were slipped, and once again I was sailing off to a new adventure. The ship soon passed Observation Island, outboard.

How quiet it seemed all of a sudden. None of my cannery friends were going my way. Gone was the camaraderie of the floater. Suddenly it seemed very empty around me. I was a little disconcerted; I hadn't remembered how alone you could feel. But I knew I would quickly make new friends. Alaska was a very friendly place, probably because so many people were alone, as I was.

The trip across Prince William Sound took me past many scenes from my recent summer. We sailed around the rocky ocean capes into Resurrection Bay, and at last the steamer sounded its throaty whistle as we approached Seward.

It seemed so strange to be on dry land again. I walked up the quiet little streets hemmed in by mountains, a typical Alaskan coastal town. Seward was an interesting place. The streets were named for U.S. presidents in the order of their election: Washington, Adams, Jefferson, and so on. I walked around a lot and finally stopped into a quiet little cafe for coffee and a chance to chat with the waitress before train time. There was plenty of time. Trains met the boats, and there was freight for all the communities to the north, including Anchorage and Fairbanks.

Trucking via the Alcan to Fairbanks was still in its infancy in 1946. Alaska Steam and the Alaska Railroad still supplied all of Alaska with everything at that time. A lot has been written about the monopoly of Alaska Steamship Company during that era, but the fact is that the Alaska Railroad, owned and run by the U.S. Government, was just as oppressive. During the 1930s the U.S. Government, at the behest of the Alaska Railroad, inaugurated a special tax on truckers delivering freight from Valdez to Fairbanks because they were undercutting the profits of the government railroad! Alaskans had many reasons to resent government from far-off Washington, D.C.

Seward was definitely a railroad town; there was only one short, stubby road out of town that led nowhere—to Kenai Lake, I think. The Alaska Railroad was the only transportation north, and I was happy to be aboard and on my way again.

The country out of Seward was mountainous and green, with dense spruce rain forests and magnificent views of peaks, lakes and glaciers, all lying in great mysterious valleys.

"Alaska Nellie" Lawing's Roadhouse on Kenai Lake was the most memorable stop. We had lunch there. Nellie Neal Lawing was another of Alaska's famous characters. I gazed at her in wonder; she was so small. Ma Pullen had been almost 6 feet tall, but Nellie was just a wisp of a woman. It was hard to believe all the stories about her: driving dog teams through blinding blizzards to find stranded train passengers in the winter; getting the mail through by dog sled when the railroad was not yet finished; and all the time running one of the most famous roadhouses along the Alaska Railroad. She used to catch Rainbow trout by fishing out the window of her roadhouse on Kenai Lake, trout that appeared on the menu that day. She was a tough and resourceful individual with a well-earned reputation. How could such a slip of a woman do all that? She wasn't any bigger than me, and at that time I weighed about 104 lbs. soaking wet, and stood barely 5 foot 2 inches. Under that tiny exterior, she was wiry and tough. How I envied her and her reputation!

Nellie was also a warm person, and when she heard I was from Denver, she wanted to talk about it, but time cut our conversation short. Both of us passed a disappointed look as I boarded the train, all too soon. I thought back, wondering what I might have told her about Denver. I remembered very little of my Denver childhood and in the manner of children, the memories were all jumbled. I doubted if Nellie's experiences would bear any resemblance to mine, anyway.

My memories as a kid were almost entirely of myself and my brother "Bus" on the streets of Denver during the Great Depression. I was always so proud of my mother, because she not only had a job (no small feat during The Depression) but one to be really proud of. She worked as a waitress in the Brown Palace Hotel, one of the finest hotels in the country. Later she worked at another extremely posh restaurant called Murphy's, where a whole wall consisted of a single tropical fish tank. Every so often, always on Saturday during slack time at the restaurant, we were invited to come and have dinner. It was impressed on us what a privilege this was. We had to bathe and dress better than for Church—more like we were being presented to the Queen of England. We were expected to act with manners becoming a young lady and gentleman, at least for the duration of the meal, and Mom would wait on us with grave dignity, looking radiantly beautiful in a crisp uniform with a fancy pink lace handkerchief in the shape of a flower pinned on her shoulder. She called us "Ma'am" and "Sir," and the little charade was a charming introduction to the kind of society that frequented the Brown Palace. We loved it.

Otherwise, we foraged and roamed the streets of Denver, and in general gained what might be called a "well-rounded" education. We lived on farms and in cities, sometimes boarded out, sometimes not; always in dingy little rooms painted beige, which we called "Tenement Tan," a color redolent with memories of cockroaches and imbedded grime. It was many years before I began to see how difficult it must have been for Mom, and what a terrific person she really was through those times. All in all, it wasn't too bad for us. We learned to be self-reliant and resourceful, to take the good with the bad, and try to treat others with respect. Mostly, my memories were pleasant.

Just out of Lawing we came to the famous "Loop District." All by itself, to see and experience this was worth the $27.25 I had paid for the ticket to Fairbanks. On the way, there was a point at which we could see the entire loop, and here we stopped and got out to look. The track took "S" turns and then did a complete loop over itself! The conductor explained that this track configuration had been necessary to get up and past the Bartlett and Deadman glaciers. We ooh-ed and ah-ed, and those of us with cameras took pictures before we all piled aboard the train again. I remember bumping my head against the window as we made the loop, trying to see the track above and then below us. It was without peer anywhere in the world. To me, the "Loop" was even more impressive than the High Bridge on the White Pass & Yukon. Later that section of track was removed when the glaciers receded.

Soon we plunged through snow sheds and tunnels and then emerged onto Turnagain Arm, where the mountains soared abruptly upward from the right side of the tracks, a region of many avalanches during certain seasons.

Then we came puffing into Anchorage station. Anchorage didn't interest me much because it was just a baby among Alaskan cities. It had not even had a gold rush! It came into being in 1914 as a railroad construction camp, and the first city lots were sold in 1920. After that it sort of settled down to a small, backwater community with only the Alaska Railroad headquarters as its basic industry.

World War II hit the town with an explosive effect, with new military bases feeding the economy. In 1946, when I passed through, Anchorage was just beginning to explode. It was emerging from its "jerkwater town" status, and there was an air of excitement that was unmistakable. Anchorage teemed with war workers and military types. In 1946 its population had soared from a thousand or so to possibly 11,000, the largest city in Alaska. As we sat in the train waiting to get under way again, it was totally unimpressive. Someone pointed out the brand new Westward Hotel with a great deal of pride. I looked up the hill to where it perched above the railroad yards—it was just a plain box-type building of three stories, nothing very spectacular at all to my big-city eyes. But I murmured approval to the seatmate who had shown it to me.

Anchorage didn't seem "adventurous" enough for my itinerary. But Nome certainly was, and I was itching to get there.

We spent the night at Curry, which was about 100 miles short of Denali National Park. When I called the big mountain "McKinley," an old sourdough in the lobby corrected me: "Yeah, I know that's what they call it, but the name of the mountain is really 'Denali.' Means 'The Great One.' Some cheechako named it after a president that never even came to Alaska, and maybe never even heard of it. It's still 'Denali' to us Alaskans."

I thought about that for a while, and decided "Denali" was certainly a more appropriate name. "Denali" seems to have more depth, respect, and poetic ring to it than "McKinley," so I adopted that style during my first year in Alaska. The Mountain, with typical disregard of our mortal mannerisms, remained lost to view by clouds. It didn't matter too much; I had seen it during my winter in Fairbanks with its summit wreathed in "sun-dogs." I knew its immortal character.

Then, after a long ride the next day, I was in Fairbanks once again, very weary, making arrangements and getting ready to board the DC-3 flight to Nome. It was quite late when I settled in and fastened the seat belt. The stewardess came down the aisle, handing out chewing gum (to ease ear pressure) accompanied by a pillow and a blanket, after the custom of the times. Also, since the flights were so long, she chatted a bit with passengers, getting acquainted. Just as steamship travel was, air travel was leisurely.

Finally, after interminable warming up of engines, we pulled to the end of the lighted runway and lifted off with a roar into the dark of night, headed for Nome.

DC-3 engines at night always looked like they were on fire. I watched these flames for a while, then suddenly I realized, one of them really was on fire! Before I could react to this knowledge, the captain's voice came on and announced we were returning to Fairbanks. Fortunately, we weren't far out. It was just one of those "mechanicals" in the air.

So there ensued another wait while the airline rustled up a spare DC-3 for us. Then once again we were winging our way through an incredibly black night toward the golden beaches of Nome.

The trips on the DC-3, as I noted before, were long. I had time to visit with the stewardess and fellow passengers while en route. My seatmate on this second flight was an interesting young fellow who said that he and his wife didn't need to mine gold; they had their own "gold mine" in Nome.

"We operate the local movie house," he explained. "Who needs a gold pan or a sluice box when you have a movie house?" That remark didn't register at the time, and was part of the general repartee and storytelling exchange that went on endlessly in those pre-television days.

Other than that, my memories of that trip are all of how dark it was. I didn't even see runway lights on the field when we landed, but I'm sure they were there. When we went into the terminal, someone was talking excitedly about a plane that crashed at the end of the runway about an hour before. I was too tired to care. Besides, I had my own "airborne mechanical" to think about.

Hello, Nome. How dark it is!

I was incredibly weary as we boarded a bus and rode through the inky blackness to Nome. It had been at least five days since I left Cordova. We were discharged in front of a hotel, which thankfully provided us with a place to park our sleepy heads for the night.

# Chapter Seventeen

## NOME: A CROSS-CULTURAL EXPERIENCE
### September & October, 1946

Dawn came and I woke to a radiantly beautiful day. All night I had heard the soft slithering of waves on a sandy shore. Anxious for my first glimpse of the Bering Sea and the "golden sands of Nome," I leaped out of bed and pulled on the nearest set of clothes so I could peek outside.

The hotel was a simple wood frame building with one long hallway down the middle and doors at each end. I headed toward the back where I assumed the ocean must be. When I opened the door I was stunned. I almost stepped into the ocean! It couldn't have been more than ten or fifteen feet away! The ocean stretched out to the far horizon from my very feet. I couldn't believe it. Later I asked people, "Don't they have any *tides* here?" One answer was: "Well yeah, maybe a foot." After the fifteen to twenty footers in Prince William Sound, that was hard to digest.

Excited, I went back to finish dressing and go out for breakfast. I stopped into the Nome Grill, the nearest restaurant, which was perched right on the beach like all the other buildings along this side of Main Street. While I was eating I asked whether they needed any waitresses. Almost immediately a short wiry guy with dark hair and a vigorous manner appeared.

"Hi, I'm Blackie. My partner, Monty Ferguson, is out of town, but he'll be back today on the plane. I hear you're looking for work?" I was hired on the spot and told to report for work about 8 o'clock that evening. It was Saturday, always a busy night.

Armed with both breakfast and a job, I ventured forth to see Nome. I walked along the beach, narrow as it was, and up and down the main drag a time or two. I remember one bar there called the "Glue Pot," which struck me as an odd name.

The town was not pretty but it had that glow of history about it, and I remember being impressed that as I stood on the beach, I was looking across the International Date Line right into tomorrow.

*Lone E. Janson*

My shift that night was normal, until 2 or 3 a.m. when the bars closed. At that time the place filled up and it was total pandemonium. There were Eskimos, servicemen, miners, local yokels and anything else you might imagine, all mixing it up and engaging in that incredible sociability that was the hallmark of Alaskans in those days. The din was deafening.

And there I was, trying to wait on everyone. I was zipping up and down, taking orders and delivering food, when someone grabbed my arm. I stopped. I had no choice.

He was a great big fellow—big around, that is—and he was feeling no pain as he slurred out: "Hi, I'm Monty Ferguson. You're the new waitress?"

I confirmed that I was and that I had to deliver this hamburger. Monty paid no attention to my protests. He had a good strong grip, and he was also having a little trouble trying not to fall off the stool, so his grip on me remained firm. He wasn't unpleasant. He was just trying to introduce himself and stay upright on his stool at the same time. I knew this was my other boss, but I had people to wait on, and he wouldn't let me go. "What the heck is this?" I wondered.

As I was wondering how to get away, his belt broke. It was not too surprising; it was a long stretch around his ample girth. He turned me loose and grabbed his pants, so I made my escape. But on my next pass by, he grabbed me again and was getting his first words out when his pants started toward the floor and he let go of me again. Even as I was hurrying and trying not to be swamped by orders, I was beginning to get a kick out of this little game. He must have tried five or six times to hold me there to talk and each time had to release me in favor of his sagging britches. Even the drunken crowd was laughing. I'll never forget Monty Ferguson. When the crowd thinned out, I had time to talk to him, and I really liked him. He was another one of those unique Alaskan characters.

It was while working at the Nome Grill that I met Phyllis Toney. My nickname was Toni, and so was hers and it led to a bit of confusion, especially since one of the cooks was also Tony. Phyllis and I became good friends and roommates for a while.

Recalling my conversation on the plane with the owner of the movie house, Toney and I went to the very next showing. Almost everybody in town attended every showing. Movies were enormously popular in post-war Nome. There was no radio or TV, so movies were the big event of the week.

The first thing Toncy and I did was buy a huge bag of popcorn. It wasn't intended so much to eat as to throw at friends to attract their attention and say "hi." Imagine my surprise when Toney grabbed a big handful and slung it as hard as she could at a couple a few rows down from us. It must have stung the backs of their necks, but they turned around and waved good-naturedly and threw some back at us. This charming custom was engaged to the point that the air looked like popcorn-snow, punctuated by shouted greetings. I could see why the manager had referred to his theatre as his "gold mine." The popcorn concession alone must have paid the overhead! The popcorn blizzard didn't subside till the cartoons that preceded the movie came on.

One rainy September day the main street turned into a sea of yellow mud. When I tried unsuccessfully to cross the street on a 1x12 plank floating precariously on the muck, my new "Penny Loafers" were adequately baptized.

If I thought Fairbanks was bad about trying to marry off young ladies, Nome was something else again. The only difference was that there were no families around to get into the act. This actually simplified the whole thing.

I was besieged by guys I knew nothing about, and I knew no one to ask about them. I quickly found out I needed no references. They generally betrayed their quality—or lack of it—immediately. There was nothing crooked or bad about most of them. They were just uninteresting, meaning they had what I define as "no character."

I went to a movie with a fellow called Carl. Carl was just one of a whole coterie of enormously dull, unattractive men who were dancing attendance on me, not for my charm but simply because I was about the only unattached young, white girl around.

Carl sort of reminded me of the Fairbanks truck driver, only he wasn't anywhere near as interesting. His popcorn-throwing arm wasn't as good as Toney's, but few arms were. But he was company to go to the movie with and have a hamburger after. Having Toney as a roommate helped; I didn't have to fight off my dates when we got home. But Toney soon decided to move on before the snow flew, so I looked around for other accommodations.

*Lone E. Janson*

I found a little cabin that I rented, and there I was introduced to the "Water Wagon" which delivered water in the winter for a price, since the water system was routinely shut off at the time of freeze-up. Another wagon that made regular rounds was the "Honey Wagon," emptying the chemical toilets we used. I am pleased to report that no one ever caught me on the John at the time they were changing the "honey buckets," an experience a friend reported happening to her in Bethel.

I liked my little cabin, and I liked Nome. As before, there were few young single women around so I had few pals, but people in general were very friendly and I was never really lonesome.

Naturally, a great many of my casual acquaintances were eligible men, but I never got close enough to any of them to have what could pass as a casual date. However, they did seem to understand my passion for the "adventurous," and that made my stay in Nome really memorable.

One time I was taken on a ride along the old tracks of some defunct railroad. We rode in a truck mounted on railroad wheels and driven in a mostly northerly direction to the location of a mine. This mine had a very unusual sluice box. Most sluice boxes I had read of were long and straight, with riffles affixed along its length to catch the heavy gold dust. This sluice box, however, was round and fixed in such a way that it could be rocked. The water apparently came in from the top and went round and round the box as it gently rocked. I didn't get to see it in operation as the gold mine had been closed since the war began. I learned that almost all gold mining had been shut down by the onset of World War II because gold was not classed as a "strategic mineral." Gold mining in Alaska never fully recovered.

Another fascinating jaunt was when I was taken for a ride to Safety Lagoon, east of Nome, by road. The road led along the cliff above the water, and was so narrow that passing another car was like a chess game. One car (usually the one on the inside) selected the widest spot possible and pulled over as far as he could. The other vehicle crept alongside till about halfway past, then stopped. Then the first vehicle eased forward and back onto the center of the road. The car on the outside had only inches to spare from the edge.

I remember the fragile beauty of arctic plants growing alongside permafrost ponds as we passed. What I remember most was the old-fashioned "ferry" across a river en route to our destination. I had never seen one of these. It was a barge affixed to a cable across the river.

We drove onto the dock and honked the horn. The lady and man came out of their house on the opposite side and proceeded to haul the barge hand-over-hand to our side. We drove aboard, and they hauled us to the other side. We paid a fee and were on our way again. I don't recall much else about that trip, except my intense pleasure at getting out of town and seeing the countryside.

Out of these forays came some strange comments between several of the gentlemen who took me on these trips. I never thought of either of them as anything but friends, but to my surprise one of them made a snide remark in my hearing about the other being "a squaw man," implying I shouldn't be seen with him. I was shocked and singularly unimpressed by this remark except for the jealous cattiness of it. Most of the Native women I had met were delightful people, and I had a hard time seeing what could be wrong with being called a "squaw man."

Our dishwasher at the Nome Grill was Eskimo, and a more charming lady I never met. We chatted whenever we had time, and one time she asked me how much they paid me per hour. Before I could answer, another waitress nudged me and shook her head. The only reason I could see for my not telling her was that they probably underpaid her something fierce. It was another impression of the rampant racism that existed in Alaska. I had run into it sort of obliquely before, but never on the scale I found in Nome. I was still very young and naive; this was my education in reality.

These were the locals. The Army was something else. I couldn't believe the predatory instincts that military service seems to instill in the male population. The one conversation I overheard among some Army guys in the restaurant was especially appalling to me. The boys were talking about the young—really young—Eskimo girl that one of them had been out with the night before. After poking fun at the buddy with a few ribald jokes, one of them asked, "Did she have a moustache?" I was shocked; this was barbaric. But I kept waiting on people and made believe I didn't hear or understand.

Nome brings back a collage of such remembered remarks, and the combination of racism and sexism they represented. I was used to the sexism, since most girls grew up with it and really had no defense against it, which partly explained why I never spoke out against it all. It would not have done any good, and probably would have made me a target. It was one of the unspoken truths of my youth, a rule you broke at your own peril. I was alone and on my own in a far part of the world. I had enough to deal with.

The fact remains that the white men I met were, well, predatory. I found the Eskimos far more interesting and delightful people than the men who were trying to impress me. The Eskimos laughed a lot, and they accepted others at face value unless you proved unworthy of such respect.

I remember walking out the road to where the King Islanders were camped, just out of town. It seems that every summer they came to Nome, turned their Umiaks upside down and draped tarps around them, and there they lived and sold their beautiful ivory carvings. I had my eye on a beautiful chess set; my brother loved to play chess. There were the white walrus ivory figures on one side and the dark fossil ivory figures on the other. I wanted to buy it, but again, I just didn't have the money. But how I did admire it! And the Eskimos—instinctively I felt their acceptance on a level I had not encountered very often anywhere. I liked these people. But I was very bashful and did not know how to relax and accept as they did. Everything was so new to me, and a little confusing.

There were exceptions to the racism among the whites, of course. One day I met and conversed with Leonard Seppala, the famous dog team driver from the Nome serum race. He served me coffee and told me stories about dog driving, and I thoroughly enjoyed the afternoon. But again, I knew so little about dog mushing that I couldn't even ask an intelligent question.

Nome had its special frontier appeal, and I had a lot of opportunity to experience it. I remember the arrival of the last boat of the season, one of the Alaska Steamship Line freighters, which lay far offshore, discharging its cargo. The first boat into Nome usually could not arrive until July, and here it was September with freeze-up expected any day. The sea was so shallow that the ship had to lay several miles out. The boat should have appeared small because of its distance, but something about the visual optics made it appear huge, the dominant thing in Nome that day.

All the freight was discharged to smaller boats, "lighters," to be carried ashore. There was a lot of it. Every family bought its next year's supplies at this time. They all ordered cases and cases of canned foods, sacks of flour and sugar, supplemental clothes and school supplies, even Christmas presents—everything for the winter. All of this had to be lightered ashore on small boats and subsequently stowed away in homes for winter. The first boat and the last boat of the season were gala affairs, once the longshoring was done.

When the ship departed, it was time for a party, and an unusual event it was! We all went swimming in the Arctic Ocean in September, just before freeze-up.

This gala swimming party bore no resemblance at all to the activities of the "6:30 Club." There were Eskimos and whites, Army and civilian, men and women alike. They built a roaring big bonfire and kept it stoked white hot. From the comfort of the fire, we'd dash into the shocking cold of the ocean, then dash back to soak up the bonfire's heat. Actually, the "swim" was more like a steam bath followed by a roll in the snow. It bordered on the insane, but it was lots of fun. Picnic-type food and hot coffee, tea and cold beer accompanied all this activity.

This grand party took place in front of Nome's new breakwater, which was pointed out to me with great pride and confidence. It was comprised of interlocking steel plates, built by the Army Engineers, I assumed. Everyone was sure it would protect the town from the fall and winter storms that occasionally decimated the town.

Winter was coming on, and I thought of the long, cold, dark winter in Fairbanks, and wondered if I really wanted another such winter so soon. Just the thought of that Fairbanks winter began to fill me with dread. I couldn't remember the beauty without remembering the depression and loneliness. I didn't know if I was really ready for another one.

About that time I got a telegram from my mother that my brother was getting out of the Navy and wishing I could be home to see him. Actually, the way she put the invitation was to include a classic cartoon of a man and woman stranded on a desert island with a single palm tree, and the woman demanding of the man: "DO something! Build a house!"

It was her way of saying "Come on home to greet your brother." I decided that was a good idea. I really wanted to see him, and besides I could begin junior college during the winter.

*Lone E. Janson*

# Chapter Eighteen

## JULI AND JUNEAU

### February 1947

On a chill 1947 February dawn, my friend Juli and I were sitting forlornly on suitcases on the Alaska Steamship Company dock in Seattle, waiting for the office to open. Behind us were a hectic 8-hour bus ride and a very blank early-morning three hours in a strange city. Ahead was Alaska and adventure. This time I knew our destination: Juneau.

Just above us, in a spanking-new coat of pearl-gray paint, the steamer Aleutian lay tied to the dock ready for the ten o'clock sailing.

I regarded that clean new coat of paint and remarked, "Looks like a big pearl-gray pair of spats."

"It's six o'clock. Two more hours before we can go aboard," said Juli. So we sat some more, making small talk and waiting.

"Yeah," I said, "I hope we can eat breakfast after we board. Or maybe we should find a small cafe nearby if any are open."

I shifted my position on the suitcase. "I wonder why they don't design suitcases a traveler can sit on?"

Juli observed, "Probably because suitcase designers never have to sit on them."

While waiting, I regaled Juli with some more stories of my adventures in Alaska. I told her of my first encounter with the Bendix washing machine in Fairbanks, a machine that was still new enough to be worth telling stories about. Somehow, that round porthole in the front where you could watch the laundry wash itself was spellbinding. The little hotel's laundry had a mangle, too, but it didn't have the charisma of the Bendix. In that machine, I had washed all the sheets, towels and pillowcases for a small hotel. I must have embellished the story a bit too much, for it was destined to cause me trouble later.

Still, it helped fill those empty hours before the steamship office opened, when things began to happen fast. Before we knew it we had breakfasted, boarded ship, and were watching the Port of Seattle drop behind.

*Lone E. Janson*

We were full of excitement, visiting and making friends all over the ship.

From among the people along the rail, a short, red-haired woman clad amply in a fur coat turned and smiled at us. The gleam of friendliness and a gold tooth in front were unmistakable, and in the easy manner of shipboard life, we soon promised to ask for the same table at mess. Marie Duvall was her name, and she was headed for Cordova. We all became good friends on that trip, especially when I told her of my Esther Island adventures.

Some time later Juli and I wandered into the salon. There were three or four young people around the piano, so we joined them for an impromptu sing-along. A young fellow in the group seemed interested in me and presently we became friendly. He seemed rather nice and a little shy, a very attractive combination. It turned out he was shy all right, shy of anything interesting to say, of opinions on anything at all, and his standard answer to any question was a vague "I don't know." Juli had been taking French and knew the phrase for that, "Je ne se pas," so that's what we called him in private. "Here comes Je Ne Se Pas, let's duck down this other passageway." There was no getting away from him, it seemed, and he was boring.

As before, I found the Inside Passage scenic and full of wildlife. Our trip included encounters with whales and porpoises, the same richly forested islands and the same clear, green-blue waters. It was so beautiful that the emotion sort of caught in your throat. I used to think, "Will there ever come a time I fail to see the magic? If I ever come to that, I'm old. If I never lose it, I'll be young forever." Nearby, a "sea parrot" (puffin), took off in a series of splashes and flew by, his orange beak looking foolishly big and bright on his stubby little black body.

Our arrival in Juneau was on a wet, foggy night. As usual, there were the crowds on the dock meeting "the boat." We went ashore and began our search for a place to live and a job to sustain us. In the interest of economy, we found a room at a broken-down place called the Home Hotel, at the end of South Franklin Street, halfway up a hill in the path of rockslides and avalanches. But we had kitchen privileges and the rent was dirt-cheap. So we moved in and went out job-hunting. We pinched pennies and combed the town for work. We shared meals and envied the newsboys, who at least had a way to make a farthing or two.

One day we passed a downtown missionary with the sign in the window that proclaimed ominously: "The wages of sin are death." I pointed the sign out to Juli and said, "Look, Juli! Wages!" We went off down the street wrapped in gales of laughter.

One day I climbed the steep hill to the Home Hotel, and Juli met me at the door, all excited. "I found you a job!" she declared.

I tried to look over my shoulder to see if there was a "Stupid" sign on my back.

Seeing none, I said: "You found ME a job?! What is this, Communism? Why didn't you find YOURSELF a job?"

"But you're experienced at this! It's the laundry in the Governor's mansion! I told Mrs. Gruening that you ran a whole laundry by yourself up in Fairbanks!"

I knew then that my big mouth had me in trouble. That "whole laundry" consisted of one single Bendix washing machine and a small hand mangle, and I did nothing but the sheets and towels for a very small hotel. My work took less than four hours a day and someone even had to show me how to run that Bendix, as I had never seen one. Now I was committed to a job I knew nothing about, reputedly "experienced," and without a chance to put the record straight. I was extremely upset, especially since I had to go to work the next morning and had not even met the people I was to work for.

As I expected, the laundry episode turned out to be a complete debacle, and an extremely embarrassing one at that. Mrs. Gruening was apparently enchanted that she had an "experienced laundress," and so she showed up while I was still trying to figure out the machines. In her arms were sofa slipcovers—mountains of them, it seemed. She deposited them and told me she needed them for a five o'clock dinner that evening. I stood open-mouthed, wondering what I had gotten into.

I looked over the slipcovers; they were heavy floral ones with ruffles at the bottom. After they were washed, all I would need to iron was the ruffles. The trouble was, I would have to sprinkle them first if I could figure out how to do that, unless I could leave the whole slipcover damp and iron them that way. As it turned out, time was pressing in on me, and I elected to leave the covers damp. I began ironing, but as soon as I'd iron a portion of ruffle, I'd look back and it was all wrinkled again, my efforts completely erased. I tried again and again, but to no avail. I had just decided I'd have to dry the whole mess and try sprinkling, when Mrs. Gruening came to get them. She was first appalled, then very angry, to see that there was no way I could get them ready in time. I had worked for hours, but they were nowhere near done. In a huff of frustration she vanished upstairs to make an emergency call to a nearby laundry. I felt terrible, but it had all been a big misunderstanding. It wasn't my fault or Mrs. Gruening's, nor Juli's either. It was just one of those things.

When that terrible day was over, Mrs. Gruening didn't want to pay me for the time spent on the slipcovers. I couldn't blame her but I had done my best in a difficult and misunderstood situation. And I desperately needed the money. I burst into tears and told her I had worked hard on those slipcovers. She relented and paid me, but of course there was no question of my coming back to work there.

Relieved, I took my small one-day paycheck and went out to buy some groceries. Poor Juli. She was really sorry about it, but it blew over quickly. Who wants to be a laundress, anyway? Not I. I wanted to be a writer, and I had already learned that all true adventures tend to be a little disconcerting. It would make a good tale to tell my grandkids, and maybe write about someday.

Juli and I both found a week or two of work as relief waitress-dishwashers at a small cafe on the waterfront run by a fellow named "Fishface Sam." As Juli observed, he had that nickname for obvious reasons.

While working there, I met a young fisherman named John. John took me down to see his fishing boat, which was very small and reeked of fish, but it seemed like another grand adventure to me. Seeing my pleasure in the boat, he offered to take me for a short ride and fired up the engine. Soon we were chugging down Gastineau Channel in the bright sunlight. It was a great ride, and I was really enjoying it as we started back up the channel for the boat harbor again. But John misjudged the channel and the boat ran aground and leaned far over to the left. I looked around. The world sure looked funny at that angle, but we were all right, and John assured me the boat would float easily again when the tide rose a little higher. So we waited. John seemed very nervous, so I asked, "Should I make us a pot of coffee while we wait?"

John said no, not while the boat was listing, then looked at me oddly. At last he said, "I thought you would get all hysterical because we went aground. I took another girl out for a ride once and she did that. Scared the bejeepers out of me."

I laughed. "Well, we're all right, aren't we? And both you and the tide book agree that we will soon be afloat, so it's just a matter of time, I guess." And so it was; we were back in port just as darkness fell. I enjoyed the adventure thoroughly.

Working at Fishface Sam's, Juli and I met another intriguing fellow named "Moose." I was beginning to really appreciate the nicknames that everyone went by in those days. It seemed your real name was not all that important. As you may have guessed, Moose was a big man, though young. Instead of being big and dumb as the stereotype has it, he was remarkably sensitive and gentlemanly. He had a part-time job as a deckhand on a fish boat, but he filled in as a singing waiter at the Red Dog Saloon. Moose and I went out a couple of times to dance; he was a great partner. I liked him but we were not really boyfriend and girlfriend. We were comfortable together, that's all.

Meanwhile, Juli and I continued our hunt for work. One nice sunny day we decided to hike out the road to see Mendenhall Glacier. We prepared a few peanut butter sandwiches, threw in a couple of candy bars, and we started hiking. It's about 13 miles each way, if memory serves. But we were young and agile and enjoyed the day. The glacier was beautiful and we oohed and aahed over the deep blue color of the glacier ice. It was not just ice-blue, it looked like someone had spilled laundry bluing there. It was dark blue.

Going and coming we passed the airport area, and watched the cows at the dairy farm there, contentedly chewing their cuds as we passed. We got very thirsty on our trip home, and finally we went up to one of the few houses we found out that way. A very friendly lady there gave us water and we visited for a while before resuming our long hike home.

About a week later, both of us landed a job at Percy's Cafe downtown, and the famine was over. It was nice to both have a job at the same place.

With the last of our funds, we went out to celebrate. As waitresses, we could count on at least some tips next day, and meals too. For this night on the town, I lent Juli my gray pin stripe suit. "Go ahead. I like that suit, it always makes me feel like a real lady when I wear it."

Juli put on the suit, and it fit her just perfectly. Juli was short, bouncy and, in that suit, looked extremely sexy. She looked at herself in the mirror and said: "There! I don't want to look like a lady. I want to look attractive!" That remark intrigued me and we got to discussing exactly what she meant by "a lady," which was someone sort of stuffy and stuck-up, while my vision of the same word meant someone very attractive and self-composed. We laughed at our different interpretations of the same word. That suit made each of us feel like our own personal ideal. In it, she was a dish, while I was a lady.

I remember going that evening to the Pamaray Club, a quiet, friendly place we both liked. It was named after the three family members who owned and operated the place: Pa, Ma, and Ray. We also went over to the Red Dog to hear Moose as a singing waiter. What Moose wanted to do was break into the nightclub circuit, and he hoped this would be a step in his career. He was good. Not only was his voice and delivery good, he also managed to crawl into the character of the singing waiter and we really enjoyed his act.

Next day we showed up at Percy's Cafe, which was a landmark in Juneau. Working there put us in contact with everyone in town, it seemed.

It was at Percy's that we met Angie, who was also a waitress there. Angie was a character, and a fun one at that. She made the time at Percy's into a picnic for me.

I enjoyed working there, but it was not so easy for Juli because one of the cooks, a Filipino named Phil, took a dislike to her, and I know from experience that an ornery cook can make a waitress' life miserable. He'd wait until Juli had an order and went to pick it up, then he'd bang his spatula down on the bell really hard and yell "Pick up!" in her ear. She'd jump and say, "My God, Phil!" Phil would laugh and laugh.

I have to admit that I liked Alaska better than Juli did. Juli had left home in the middle of a romantic tiff with her boy friend, and between the torment dished out by Phil and the love letters coaxing her, she soon decided to go back home.

Waiting for Juli's boat, which left about three a.m., we made the rounds again. Moose had moved on, hopefully to better things, a new gig somewhere. Now Juli was leaving too. I felt really sad as I waved goodbye to her and the ship glided gracefully around a point.

Juli was married shortly after she returned home. Within a few years they had a fine family and were very happy by the time I lost track of her during my wanderings. Lost track, that is, until the day, 45 years later, Bob and Juli Larson were passing through Anchorage, spotted my name in the phone book and called me. I went out to the airport to visit as they waited for their plane, and it was wonderful to relive old times again.

*Lone E. Janson*

# Chapter Nineteen

## WAITRESSING IN ALASKA
### April 1947

After Juli left, Angie and I worked together on the night shift at Percy's. Actually it was what they called the "swing shift," from six to two. Early in the evenings and on weekends, Percy's was a teenage hangout. The restaurant served sandwiches and light meals, and there was a really fine soda fountain.

Mostly, the teenagers were well behaved, or at least as well behaved as their high sex drive and soaring energy allowed them to be. I was technically still a teenager myself, but I had been on my own too long to think of myself in that fashion.

On one particular Saturday, the crowd of teenagers was really big and very high-spirited just after the matinee let out. Percy's was packed. We were running, literally running, to keep up. There was a booth full of about six very boisterous teenagers, and I served them water and menus while I went on to other customers.

When I came back they were gone. But Angie pointed out that they were in the next booth, watching. They were suspiciously quiet. I went to clean up the booth where they had been and discovered they had turned over the glasses with the water still in them. It's a neat trick, but I came from a waitress family and had learned several ways to deal with a full water glass that is upside down. I could have just slid the glass to the edge of the table where it would dump harmlessly into a bowl, but those kids were right in the next booth, waiting to see the fun. So I decided to give them some fun.

I picked the first glass up quickly and aimed in the direction of the next booth, where it sprayed all over them.

While they were still gasping in surprise, I said, "Oh, I'm so sorry! I'll get a towel for you!" and off I went to get the towels. They still didn't say anything as I continued to lay the "so sorry" bit on them and distributed towels, but they knew exactly what had happened. A day or two later another teenager came in and said to me, "I hear you are the waitress who is 'the business.'" I just smiled and gave him a glass of

*Lone E. Janson*

water and a menu. None of them ever pulled that stunt on me again.

One of Percy's leading items was Strawberry Shortcake, which we served with the exact number of strawberries prescribed by Percy, covered with mountains of fake foamy whipped cream from a spray can. Very popular. When we had special customers, if Percy wasn't around, we liked to sneak a few more strawberries onto the shortcake; but Angie pointed out "Percy might be watching."

Her eyes would twinkle, and a half-smile twitch around her mouth, a sure sign that she'd come up with something really witty.

"Did you ever notice that the walls here are beige, and Percy has a habit of wearing beige shirts?" Angie waited for that to sink in, then added: "He's wearing camouflage so he can catch us putting too many strawberries on the shortcake!"

Our shifts required cleaning up at the end of the day, since we closed the place. One of our customers was Bob, the taxi driver, who had a habit of coming in late after we had already scrubbed the place down.

"Wouldn't you know he'd want a milk shake after the fountain is all washed down and closed?" one of us would say.

"Just want to see you girls earn your pay, that's all," Bob would say with a straight face, getting into the spirit of the thing.

"Don't you know those things make you fat? Look, Angie, he's got a spare tire already. Middle-aged spread?"

"No," said Angie, "That's just his money belt."

"You're just jealous. Laugh and grow fat," Bob would grin, slurping his milk shake.

It was Angie who came up with the cleverest witticisms, unexpected and hilarious. It was Angie who would offer a prize for the biggest cockroach of the evening. And it was usually my boyfriend, McGee, who won the prize, lining them up, hour after hour, in front of him. This was late at night, of course.

Cockroaches were very much a part of early Alaska. They would have been easy to get rid of if you didn't mind freezing up all the plumbing in the building, but short of that it was a constant battle, a little (actually, totally) on the losing side, to control them.

McGee was the first fellow I really recognized as being a "boyfriend." What I mean is, someone very attractive to me and apparently attracted to me as well. He was a control tower operator at the airport, and if he was on duty next day, he could not drink anything alcoholic. So he sat there night after night waiting for me to get off work, and drinking coffee by the gallon for hours. Of course, after a certain number of hours and cups of coffee, he tended to make a lot of trips to the back of the cafe.

Angie was in Seventh Heaven. All her humorous talents came to play on the hapless McGee. "Bee Line McGee," it started out, but soon she adopted "McGoo," after my favorite cartoon of those days, the "Near-sighted Mr. McGoo."

Poor "Bee-Line McGoo" became the object of all of Angie's powers of teasing. He was a really nice boyfriend, and patient beyond belief, or else he could never have survived Angie.

He gave back as good as he got in the teasing department. He exchanged the same type of repartee with us as Bob did. It was kind of expected, and it made the long nighttime hours go faster.

Cockroach contests weren't all that Angie dreamed up. There was the canned milk poetry contest. After my stint on the White Pass & Yukon, "armored cow" was considered fair game for such a contest.

Some of the poetic entries were borderline obscene. The first prize verse exceeded all limits, but was still so funny it had to take first prize. It went:

*"No tits to pinch,*
*No shit to pitch,*
*Just stick a hole in the Son of a Bitch!"*

The first prize was probably the biggest cockroach of the evening. No wonder I enjoyed working at Percy's.

Because McGee was a control tower operator, I learned that airplane landings and takeoffs were under a system called "Ground Controlled Approach," or GCA. It's probably totally obsolete nowadays, but it fascinated me as he explained it. Basically, it was all controlled by radio contact with the plane.

"What do you do about planes that have no radio?" I asked, and in answer, McGee brought out "The Light." It had sights on it like a rifle would have. He could pinpoint the plane that was approaching by

*Lone E. Janson*

lining it up in the crosshairs, and he'd push either the red or the green button, and the plane was supposed to peal off and not land if he got the red signal, but was clear to land if it was green.

While he was showing me this process, there was a plane taxiing out for takeoff, and also one on final approach. One of them had no radio, so I got an immediate demonstration.

"Let's see if this guy's paying attention," said McGee. He flashed the red light at the approaching plane, and immediately it pulled up and turned away for another go-around. The taxiing plane was then cleared for takeoff. I found the tower and its procedures very interesting.

Spring was coming, and both Angie and I wanted to move on. I wanted to go back to Fairbanks and look for a summer job in the Bush, and Angie decided to join me. I was happy about that, because it was a lot more fun to travel with a buddy than alone, and Angie was such fun to be around. So we gave notice to Percy and in a couple of weeks were ready to fly to Fairbanks. As we lifted off the runway at Juneau airport, McGee flashed the green light to me. I'll never forget that. It was really a sweet gesture of goodbye.

When you travel sort of "off-the-cuff" like I was doing, every visit to the same place seems entirely different. This time Fairbanks had another aspect, it seemed. First we had to find a place to live. We found a room for rent in a private house, and it was here that I really became aware of the water problem in Fairbanks. Fairbanks water was HARD; it left stains in bathtubs, in sinks, in washing machines, and on clothes. The landlady here said that she even put a small amount of soap in the rinse water to prevent gradual staining of her clothes. The theory was that the bit of soap took the staining materials into suspension.

Drinking tap water was distinctly unpleasant. Suburban Fairbanks was served by water wagon, which dispensed purified water to residences for a price. Certain places had soft water wells, but not many. Our landlady discouraged taking too many baths because of the water situation. Angie cracked jokes endlessly about Mrs. G almost having a heart attach because we took a shower that day.

Mrs. G also had a Husky that she kept tethered on a stout chain out in the yard. That was the meanest-looking Husky dog I ever saw. He looked at you like he'd like to snap your head off. But the funny thing was that he was the gentlest creature on earth. I never saw him hurt a

*Lone collects water from the water wagon in Fairbanks.*
Photo by Angie Bennett Olson.

*Lone E. Janson*

fly, and it turned out neighbor kids played with him all the time.

On the other hand, when we walked out toward the end of town (which is practically downtown nowadays), there were a number of sled dog teams, each dog tied securely to his individual house out of reach of each other. THESE dogs were not to be trifled with, and snarled and strained to get at us when we passed.

We looked for work at all the usual places, especially looking for a job out in the "boonies" somewhere—a mining camp or something. But we were having no success.

One day I got a card from George Prater asking if I was going to come to work on the floater again that summer. Angie and I looked at each other and decided, why not? I dropped a post card to Prater, "I'll take the job, and save one for my friend."

Angie and I were running low on funds by now, so we decided to hitchhike to save bus fare. We wouldn't want to pack suitcases along, so we would ship them by bus to Valdez. That would be cheaper than fares.

We actually had no inkling of what we were getting into, or how to survive in the wilderness. We really expected to get rides all the way. After all, it was a main highway, and nobody passed up hitchhikers in those days. But the truth is that traffic was not one of the Richardson Highway's problems. We might see three cars in an entire day, if we counted those going both directions. We didn't know this.

We figured we might have to hike part of the way, but if worse came to worse, we thought we could build a campfire and camp out in the mountains. "I've got a lighter!" said Angie. And I was naive enough to think that was all it would take—a lighter to start a fire, and a brown bag of extra food. It turned out later that the lighter didn't even work!

When we started out, we didn't have a warm coat or a sleeping bag, let alone a blanket. We had no tent, no protection from the elements, nothing with which to cut firewood. We figured, what the heck, it was nearly summer!

Angie told me later that she simply had no idea of the distances and wildness of the country. She was thinking in terms of hitchhiking in the "Old Country," maybe ten miles or so. But the fact was, we were setting out on a journey of 400 miles that crossed three mountain ranges with distances of twenty to forty miles between roadhouses. It was usually a three-day drive in an automobile.

My only excuse was that I had no experience in outdoorsman-ship. I had been safely insulated inside of a nice warm bus on my first trip in that direction.

But we had our lighter, our innocence, and a brown paper bag full of food, so we set out.

At the local water wagon we had our picture taken with Angie's camera as we toasted our proposed trip with distilled water in paper cups.

*Lone and Angie toasting the beginning of their journey to Valdez.*

*Angie Bennett and Lone getting ready to hitchhike the Richardson Highway.*

*Lone E. Janson*

# Chapter Twenty

## LONG HITCH ON THE RICHARDSON

### May 1947

Angie and I hiked about a mile out the road before we got our first ride. It was a truck with a man and woman in it, headed for Black Rapids Roadhouse. They were proprietor and cook for the roadhouse, probably man and wife.

"Mind riding in the back?" they asked. We said no, and jumped aboard. It was a flatbed with short side rails and a few 50-gallon drums of stove oil held in place with a strap. The roads were bumpy so Angie threw one leg over this strap as a sort of brace. She opened our brown bag and got out a sandwich—bologna with lots of mustard. She just had her mouth open to take a bite when it happened.

Inside the truck the man said to his wife, "I think I'll give the girls a thrill," and took the corner a little too fast, something decidedly unsafe on the old Richardson gravel trail. The truck hit a soft shoulder and went over on its side in the ditch. I was thrown into some soft sand, unhurt, but one of the oil drums fell on Angie's leg and left a big bruise and welt that lasted for years afterward. Luckily, nothing was broken, but her hand and face were full of mustard. I was glad she hadn't smeared ketchup on her sandwich; I probably would have thought it was blood. She looked funny covered with yellow "blood." Angie and I seemed to have fared slightly better than the driver and his wife. There was no sound coming from the truck cab and that alarmed us. We went to look inside, in time to see both of them shaking their heads as if just coming to. They must have both been momentarily stunned.

As they climbed out, we looked around. We were in the middle of nowhere, wilderness all around. Then suddenly, out of the woods stepped this Indian. He asked if anyone was hurt, and told us there was an Army rest camp just down the road, about half a mile. Then, seeing that everything was okay, he vanished into the woods just as mysteriously as he had appeared.

*Lone sits behind the driver and cook after the truck accident on the Richardson Highway.*

Other than her badly bruised leg, Angie's only other injuries were the mustard makeup and a big rip in the back of her pants. She tied her thin raincoat around her waist to cover it while we all hiked down to the rest camp. The boys at the camp welcomed us and built a campfire to cook on. Then one of them went back with the truck owner to help get the vehicle out of the ditch and the drums of stove oil reloaded. In the meantime we cooked some lunch, or rather, the lady cook from Black Rapids did most of the cooking. We ate a good meal there.

There was a little lake at this rest camp, and I was climbing around the edge of it when I slipped and fell in. I crawled out, teeth chattering, and one of the Army guys found a raincoat to wrap around me while we dried my clothes next to the campfire. When I walked around in that big, long raincoat, the only thing that seemed to move was my two little feet at the bottom. Angie laughed, "You look like a tank!" So she whipped out her camera and got a picture of Toni the Tank. Meanwhile our lady cook had found some mending equipment and Angie was able to sew up her pants.

With all this excitement, we were getting a little tired, and my clothes were drying anyway, so three of the Army guys graciously gave

*"Toni the Tank"*                                    *Photo by Angie Bennett Olson*

us and the lady cook their bunks so we could take a nap. The bunks were well draped with mosquito netting as protection from the "Alaska Territorial Birds," mosquitoes.

A little later we were on our way again to Black Rapids. Great gray clouds of dust rose from the road, and settled over the two of us in the

*Lone E. Janson*

back. We finally came to Black Rapids where we got off, looked at each other and burst out laughing—we were totally gray with dust.

Later, as we prepared to leave the Black Rapids Roadhouse, the lady cook's parting remark was, "I think you girls are nuts, but send me some pictures!"

After Black Rapids we started hoofing it up into the first range of mountains. As we hiked along, the only living thing we saw for quite a while was a porcupine. He rustled his quills at us and waddled off the road. We wanted to stop and build a fire, and that's when we discovered the lighter didn't work. We didn't even have a match!

Angie had been looking down the mountainside at the rivers, still ice-covered, and thinking about how blithely she and I had planned to camp out overnight in the mountains. She had only a thin raincoat, and I had a light summer jacket. All we had was a small lunch, which we called "The Baby," since someone had to carry it. "Shall I carry The Baby for a while now?" we'd ask from time to time.

We had been hiking for several hours without seeing a single car. That's when I began to realize that the Richardson Highway in those days was not exactly what you'd call busy.

At last we saw a dust cloud approaching. We turned to face this lone automobile and stuck our thumbs out. The car had two guys in it, and came to a screeching halt in another big cloud of dust. Their surprise at seeing two girls out here in the middle of the wilderness was apparent. They gaped at us, and demanded, "What are you two doing here?"

I began to chuckle, because suddenly I had this vision:

I could see us, the first hitchhikers on the moon, being picked up by some hi-tech moon buggy, trailing clouds of dust behind it. The two drivers of this moon-vehicle, gaping and demanding, "What are you two doing here?" Come to think of it, we might have looked like moon people, too. We were so dust-covered that no color of any sort was apparent on us. We were "gray ghosts" I guess.

I was still chuckling to myself at this vision as we clamored into the car. We really were colorless. I explained to them, "She's a blonde and I'm a brunette!" They just gaped some more.

We were very tired by this time, especially me. I rode in the back seat of the car, totally exhausted—too tired to even talk. Besides, in the back seat on a gravel road it's almost impossible to hear the conversation in front. Angie, in the front seat, was telling the story of our adventures. Finally, the driver said, "Your girl friend in the back seat is awfully quiet." I roused myself enough to declare: "I'm the strong, silent type!"

That got everyone laughing and I didn't have to do much talking. These fellows took us as far as Sourdough Roadhouse. At one of our coffee stops along the way, a waitress asked us: "Aren't you worried about riding with those guys?" and I answered, "Oh, I think we can handle them!" The truth is, no one we met on the Richardson ever made a pass or did anything that was even slightly out of line. I think the two of us looked so tough, covered with gray dust and windblown, that no one would want to get funny.

But that didn't mean things couldn't be misinterpreted. While riding with these fellows, they had stopped on the plateau outside of Fairbanks. The driver turned and asked, "Do you girls want to pay the rent now?"

Angie's jaw dropped, and seeing her horrified look the driver protested, "No, no, no! All I wanted to know is if you wanted a rest stop here." So we got out and found a couple of convenient bushes to function as wilderness rest rooms.

The manager at the Sourdough Roadhouse started to put us in the same rooms with the two guys, and I was protesting, "They're with us, but they're not WITH us!" Finally, they fixed up a couple of cots for Angie and I, out in a little cabin. While we ate dinner, the bus came in with our suitcases aboard. So at least we had a change of clothes, but sent the suitcases on again with the bus the next morning. When we went to take a shower there was only cold water, so we took a shower in that. We were very tired, and conked out for the count. We slept so hard that when we woke up, we were hoping we wouldn't get charged for another day. Our finances couldn't stand up to that.

We rode the rest of the way to the Glennallen cutoff with these fellows, and here we said goodbye and began to hike again. We walked all the way from there to Copper Center Lodge, a distance of about 17 miles, without seeing another car. It was a quite a long hike, but the weather was warm, and we were young, sturdy, and I guess dumb enough to be in this situation. At Copper Center Lodge, we paid for

*Lone E. Janson*

two baths. I took mine while Angie sat over coffee and talked to the lady manager. When I came out, the lady said, "There are a couple of truck drivers here going into Valdez. Maybe you can get a ride with them." Knowing how little traffic we could hope to see, we jumped at the chance. We asked, and the guys said sure, but they were leaving right away. Angie never got her bath, which was already paid for. They were going as far as Tonsina Lodge that night. They would start very early the next day for the rest of the drive on into Valdez.

At Tonsina we made very sure to get up early enough to ride with the truckers into Valdez. This time, as we came down off Three-Mile Hill toward Keystone Canyon, we drove along the newly opened section of roadway in the bottom of the canyon. I told Angie of my trip last year along the horse-and-buggy trail, plainly visible above us high up on the canyon wall. How different this trail was! Shortly after that, we were in Valdez.

Valdez last year had been extremely boring, but this time it was not. In fact, it was sort of off-the-wall, almost unrealistic, mostly due to Angie's company.

The truck drivers offered to buy us lunch, and we accepted if we could bathe and dress first. When we emerged, the truck drivers didn't even know us without our dust. This time I didn't have to explain who was blonde and who, brunette.

We went down to a little cafe run by Nils Anderson. It was boat day, and there were lots of people in town, but just for an hour or two. While we had our meal there, a group of teenagers came into the cafe. They were the same high-spirited hooligans from Percy's that we were trying to get away from when we left Juneau! We began to exchange stories, even laughing about the water glass incident. We went down to the dock to see them off on the Alaska.

After that, Angie and I went to find out about the plane to Cordova, and as before, it would be there in a few days, weather permitting. We looked over our dwindling pile of money and decided to try to find some waitress work while we waited. The next day we went back to Nils' cafe for that purpose.

When we walked in this time it was obvious that something was wrong. Nils was in a state of shock, waiting on customers and trying to cook while sipping whiskey out of a coffee mug. It turned out that the

Alaska sailed with more passengers than our teenage mob. Nils' wife (who was the waitress) had run off with his cook, leaving by the only transportation available, the boat.

Naturally, Nils jumped at the chance to put us to work. We waited tables and fry cooked, and we also decided to make some pies and cakes, since there was no bakery in Valdez. Angie would make the pies and I'd make a cake.

While we were doing this, Nils kept going uptown and bringing in customers. Angie pulled me aside and asked, "Do you notice anything funny going on?"

I looked around the room. The counter was full of young guys, all sitting there, practically with a fork in one hand and a knife in the other, waiting for the pies and cakes to get done. Truly, there was no bakery in Valdez!

Angie went on, "Do you notice how they are all young, eligible guys? You know what I think? That foxy old Nils! He's trying to get a romance going between one of us and one of them so we won't go to Cordova to work on the floater. He thinks that will keep at least one of us here!" I went on mixing the cake batter and looked again. By golly, I think she was right!

We both broke into almost uncontrollable giggles. Soon Nils came in with another candidate, and also a bottle of some rotgut liquor called "King's Treasure." We tried a sip of it, and we both agreed it tasted like furniture polish. No chance of either of us getting drunk on that gunk.

When the pies came out of the oven, the forks and knives got very busy and the pies vanished in very short order. By then my cake was done and I was trying to concoct some "seven-minute" frosting, which did not turn out at all. It stubbornly remained just syrupy goo. I wailed, "Look at this! I can't put that on the cake!"

A chorus of young male voices came back: "Sure you can! Just pour it right on there!" I poured it on, and the cake soaked it up like a thirsty sponge. It looked awful, but the cake also vanished down hungry male throats in nothing flat, and no complaints at all.

As we finished up our shift that night, Angie said, "Better eat good. I have this funny feeling we won't get paid!" We dug out steaks and made ourselves a feast. Good thing, because Nils himself left town the next day and no one knew exactly where he went. Probably to find his wife and the cook.

We didn't care. The plane came winging in over Valdez harbor that day. We were on hand watching it as it circled and circled, as if deciding whether to land or not. We got a little nervous waiting, but finally it landed on the water and Mudhole Smith, the pilot, climbed out and was holding his plane against the wind, waiting to load and take off as quickly as possible. Jarvi, the clerk, carried Angie out to the plane while I waited my turn. From her seat onboard, Angie snapped a picture as Jarvie returned to carry me out to the plane.

*The ticket agent in Valdez carrying Lone to the plane for the trip to Cordova.*

Lone E. Janson

# Chapter Twenty-One

## RED SALMON SEASON, BERING RIVER
### June 1947

Each year, the first commercial salmon season in Alaska is always the one on the Copper and Bering rivers, near Cordova. It's the earliest run of King and Red salmon. Parks Floater #1 was already at Bering River when Angie and I arrived in Cordova.

*Lone standing on shore at Bering River with the Floating Cannery in the background.*

We were taken across the Copper River Flats to Bering River, where the familiar barn-red floater was moored next to a steep ridge of mountains. Across the muddy Bering River lay flat grassland fronting on Bering Glacier, which was plainly visible from the floating cannery.

As soon as we arrived, I had a wonderful surprise: Marian Arnold was also aboard! She hadn't been just kidding last year when she told me that if she hadn't already taken the Barrow job, she would have come with me to Cordova. Here she was, on the floater! Angie, Marian and I became fast friends. We made signs to put on the women's dorm,

*Ladies exercising.*

announcing that this was "The Snake Den." We did morning calis-
thenics, played tricks on one another and members of the crew, and in
general enjoyed great high spirits. We were everywhere, on foot along
the shore, or on the boats, learning about this fascinating new section
of the country. We had picnics on the roof of the cannery scow, where
we jumped rope and played all sorts of goofy games. We soon became
known as "The Wonder Girls," as in "I wonder what they'll do next."

The "Mad Hansens," Mae, Dora, and Louise, were also here, also
a number of women from the year before, including Lil Beyer, so we
really had a crew destined to have fun. A couple of the Hansen brothers,
Roy and Ed, were fishing for the floater, and of course I knew them
from last year at Esther Island.

The fishermen often caught small Dungeness crabs in their nets, so
we salvaged some from the boats that were delivering to the floater, and
stashed them under the covers of Lil Beyer's bed. The resultant uproar
filled us with glee, even though the crabs showed up in our own bunks
the next day, with just as much uproar, this time to Lil's delight.

It was Marian who put us up to that, but I must admit we were
readily open to such suggestions. I was beginning to learn more about
Marian's background in the Swedish merchant marine. Her skipper
had remarked that as a seaman she was worth "lots of buckets of gold."

Marian came from a large family. Such was her upbringing that when each of the kids came of age, it was a tradition for their father to take them out and get them drunk.

The type of fishing here in Bering River was different from what I had observed the year before. The summer season on Prince William Sound is primarily a seine fishery, while this was a drift gillnet fishery. Simply put, a purse seine is a huge net that wraps around a school of fish, and purses up at the bottom. A drift gillnet snares the fish mostly by the gills. Here on the muddy Bering River the fellows would run upstream and lay out their drift gillnets and float back downriver. The fish would hit the nets underwater and "gill" there. The fishermen then picked the fish out of the net.

Technically, drifting in the river itself was illegal. I was on the floater for almost two weeks before I knew that. Everyone drifted Bering River. One day Mr. Prater stood by the window watching the boats drift by, when someone said: "Isn't it illegal for those boats to drift gillnet in the river like that?" Prater looked innocently at the perpetrator of such a remark, and said: "What boats? I don't see any boats."

It underscored the attitude that Alaskans had toward federal control of Alaska's fisheries. The fishermen were convinced that the big canning companies were ripping off the Territory royally, devastating the fisheries, paying almost no taxes, fighting statehood and local control, and in many cases keeping residents from cashing in on their own resources. So Alaska fishermen were engaged in the biggest protest movement since the Boston Tea Party. It was a page right out of Thoreau's "Passive Resistance." Illegal fishing was not only condoned, but encouraged, because it was perceived as the only way we could gain control of our own fisheries. So declared the fishermen in our many gabfests and coffee klatches aboard the boats.

This new country fascinated me. Bering Glacier, I learned, was one of the largest glaciers outside of Greenland, but we saw only the distant blue-white snout of one lobe of it. Just a little distance downriver was the site of an old Indian village called Chilkat. Little was left of that village site, but just a tad farther downriver were the bleached remains of an old cannery, where one day a whistler (marmot) sat and whistled at me. He was almost the same silvery color as the wood he sat on, and because of a strange optical illusion, he looked almost as big as a bear.

*Lone E. Janson*

I liked to walk along the shore of the river and study the rocks and plants there. At one point along the riverbank I found odd round rocks imbedded in the country rock; they were "concretions." In this same area a few years later I found a fossilized dinosaur egg! Mostly what I found, though, were beautiful Alaskan wildflowers. At the site of Bering River's Chilkat, I found nettles growing. The Mad Hansens told me you always found nettles growing on the site of old cabins or villages, and rarely anyplace else.

We were in the dining hall visiting one evening when someone made a motion to be quiet and come to the window. We did, and there was a fairly large blackie (black bear) cruising up and down the beach, looking things over. The next day a maintenance man was working near the floater and saw the bear again.

After that, because of this new danger, Mr. Prater cut our forays along the shore short. From then on we had to confine our roaming to outings on the skiffs or the boats that fished for us. Or stay home, which was not in our natures.

Because of the "bear ban" concerning going ashore, Roy and his

*Group at Katalla, with the "Mad Hansens."*

*Marian Arnold (left) and Angie Bennett (right) with Bill Hansen at his home in Katalla.*

brother Ed took me on a number of skiff-and-kicker jaunts. Once we went out to Okalee Spit to watch the fishing and to see the seals along the spit; seals were overrunning the flats in those days. A lot of the fish coming through the filler were so badly mangled by seals that they had to be discarded. The seals didn't eat the whole fish, only the choice parts like eyeballs, and mangled the rest so that they were just waste. They frequently destroyed as many as a hundred fish in a gillnet, eating only a few bites from each one.

Roy and Ed were Alaska Natives of Tlingit descent from the Katalla area, so it was traditional for them to conduct a spring seal hunt. Roy's seal hunt included a trip upriver to Bering Lake, complete with tour-guide type of information. He showed me the coal seams at the head of Bering Lake where the black deposits were plainly visible from the water. Then the skiff roared downriver past the Chilkat site, and down to the old cannery, and on to Softuk Bar where he shot a seal. The seal floated long enough to be retrieved easily.

Roy explained that they hunted seals in spring instead of fall because in the spring they are fatter. They tend to float long enough to prevent much of the waste that accompanies fall hunting. "In fall the seals tend to sink like a rock and it is very hard to salvage your animal."

*Taking boat trips broke the boredom. Here, two of the Hansen sisters, Dora and Louise.*

Roy also talked of the waterproof quality of seal fur, and its beautiful creamy speckled markings. It was highly prized by Natives in this rainy area, as was also the liver.

"Seal liver is the best liver there is," said Roy. "Better than calves' liver or any other on the market." After trying it, I had to agree.

Roy and Ed were both trappers in the wintertime when there was no cannery work or commercial fishing. They usually engaged in this trade at Katalla where their dad, the elderly Bill Hansen, lived. We had occasion to make at least one short trip to Katalla that summer, where we poked around in the sagging and abandoned buildings of that ghost town. While there, I took pictures of Angie and Marian with old Bill Hansen at his cabin.

One weekend a group of us got together for a trip over to the flats to see the old locomotive there. I couldn't believe there could be a locomotive out here, fifty miles from the nearest civilization, but the Hansens explained that in the early days, when they were trying to develop the coal mines in this area, this little railroad had been called "Bering River Railroad." The old-timers affectionately named the engine itself "Ole." The place we landed our skiff was called "Goose City." Our party trudged through tall grass toward the clearly visible Bering Glacier, and very soon came upon the abandoned "Ole" on Bering River Flats. We pulled out our picnic lunches and spent a delightful sunny afternoon near the engine. Roy even climbed into the smokestack!

Again, the season was not too busy. Rainy days kept us confined, as it was a rainy climate here. As always when you are out in the boonies,

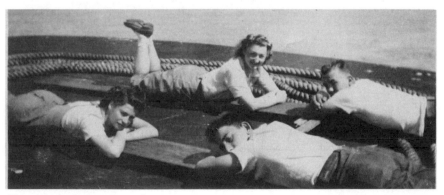

*Slow times led to boredom.*

cabin fever threatened. I remember listening to the radio schedule when Mr. Prater reported: "There's nothing here but a bear, and he went over the mountain!"

Boredom began to hang over us like a pall. So one Saturday afternoon Angie, Marian and I got our heads together and decided to have an impromptu dance. We couldn't do it halfway, it had to be something really off-the-wall. So we decided we'd dress in the most

*Lone with stick partner at the "Mop Dance."*

*Lone E. Janson*

outlandish costumes we could dream up on the spur of the moment and present ourselves as country hicks coming over here to this "big city" floater for a dance.

All of us elected to go with pigtails in our hair. Angie's hair not only had pigtails, but rag curlers too. Marian's costume featured a torn T-shirt, and mine was a blend of long underwear under bib overalls, the "long johns" showing at top and bottom. It really grieved me they weren't the traditional red underwear, so I substituted a red kerchief hanging out of my hip pocket. To complete our outfits, we all wore hip boots or cannery boots. Surveying one another, we began to really get into the spirit of the thing, so we decided it was to be represented as a "formal" dance, so over all these crazy duds we donned bathrobes that we "country hicks" thought were formal gowns. The goofiest hats we could find topped off the entire effect.

*Marian, Angie and Lone (peeking from under the pile) at the Mop Dance.*

We waited for just the right moment, when most of the crew was gathered in the dining hall playing solitaire or visiting. It was very quiet in there; people were getting bored. We had been on the floater for about a month by then, and the bears had confined us most of the time to the floater itself.

*Lone E. Janson*

Into this bucolic scene we three wild hooligans came roaring, laughing and yelling, "Hey, here we are, over from Goose City to the formal dance here on the Big City Floater! Yup! Yessirree-bob."

Jaws dropped. Then the laughter began as we showed off our "formal attire." We posed and mugged, showing how elegant our "bathrobe formals" were. Then we peeled off the boots and robes and got to the crazy underpinnings with rolled up pant legs and bare feet designed for dancing.

*At the Mop Dance. From the right: Mae Hansen, Angie and Marian. Lone on the left.*

It was amazing how fast the spirit of the thing caught on. Before we knew it, while we were still talking "hillbilly" and cracking atrocious jokes and puns, the tables got folded up, a phonograph appeared and records started playing. It was an evening of crazy dances, featuring the mop dance where one of us danced with the mop till we got tired of it and threw it on the floor. That was the signal to grab another partner and the leftover person to dance with the mop.

When I got the mop, I had to ham it up by grabbing a jug of cleaning fluid and really putting on a show with my new boy friend "Mop-head Jones," and his moonshine jug. Everyone was acting crazy like this and laughing so hard that the next day most of us had sore muscles from laughing. It was a wonderful, spontaneous evening, with lots of dancing, laughing and clowning around. That crazy dance was the highlight of my cannery career. With Angie and Marian carrying the spirit of it, everyone joined in and had a wonderful time.

When the seining season was set to open in early July, the floater was towed to Esther Island with the whole crew still aboard. Between ourselves, we figured that they wouldn't let us go to Cordova because they figured we'd quit, and they needed a crew too badly to risk it.

It was a beautiful trip across the Copper River Flats into Prince William Sound and once again clear across the Sound to Esther Island. How happy I was to be headed back to my "old homestead."

*Lone E. Janson*

# Chapter Twenty-Two

## ESTHER ISLAND—2ND SUMMER

### July & August, 1947

As we rounded the point into Mink Bay, I saw the Minker, just as beautiful as ever, tracing a perfect circle in the water as it scurried to position itself for its next task.

There was my beautiful waterfall again, set in the green majesty of Esther Island's sea and forest. There can hardly be any place on this planet as beautiful as "Mink Bay" on Esther Island. It was so good to

*Lone taking a break.*

*Lone E. Janson*

*Helen and Martin Andersen.*

be home—but were the gnats and mosquitoes this bad last summer, I wondered?

One thing remained the same: the 6:30 Club picked right up where it left off the year before, the three of us out swimming every morning before breakfast. This year I was put in the warehouse on the box stitcher from the beginning.

I was standing at the stitcher doing my thing on a Saturday morning when everyone else was working on the can line. I was all alone in the warehouse when Martin Anderson came in and saw me. I knew Martin Anderson well. He was married to another of the "Mad Hansen" sisters. Helen and Martin had the Lady Jane, and Martin was just about the biggest cut-up in the fleet. No joke seemed too outrageous to Martin.

He came over to me, his eyes dancing with mischief and said, "I'll give you a dollar if I can throw you overboard right now!"

Quickly I whipped off my glasses and watch and said, "Show me the dollar!" When he produced it I grabbed it and went over to the edge of the scow where he gave me a shove. I had a nice little swim, and climbed back aboard a dollar richer.

I was stitching away, dripping on the boxes, when George Prater came along. He didn't say anything, just shook his head in wonder. I was one of the "Wonder Girls" anyway. I thought that was a pretty easy dollar and a good swim to boot.

I kept on stitching and soon another young fisherman came wandering through, his rolled towel and soap under his arm, looking for the showers.

"Hey," I called to him. "Give me a dollar and you can push me overboard!"

The fisherman blinked a couple of times, and said, "Wh-why would I want to do that?"

"Aw, come on, be a sport!" I urged him.

He could see that the easiest way to get rid of this madwoman was to produce a dollar and shove me in, so he did. He stood on the edge watching me swim around like a seal, shook his head and went his way. People seemed to do a lot of head shaking over me in those days. Little did I know, fate had just given me a look at my future, for I would one day marry this man.

The warm sunny days often lured the crew ashore for a wiener

*Picnic and swim at Esther lake.*

roast over a campfire, followed by a hike up to Esther Lake for a swim. The lake had a large rock at the closer end, near the waterfall, and the rock sort of created a warmer, shallower swimming hole for those who were less proficient in the water. From the rock, we "6:30-ers" liked to dive into the deeper water on the other side. One day while I was swimming there, a plane circled and landed. It had the word "Chris"

*Lone swimming out to meet a plane on Esther Lake.*

on the pontoon, and when the prop stopped, I swam out to talk to the pilot. It was Haakon "Chris" Christensen asking me about the fishing in Esther Lake. Because of the big waterfall, Esther Lake had no fish at all as far as I knew, only a small bunch of Dolly Varden at the pond partway down. One of the crew took a picture of me swimming out to the plane. In later years Christensen Air Service merged with Mudhole Smith's Cordova Airlines.

Sometimes just Angie, Marian and I went up to the lake to swim. We all brought our suits along and changed into them down by the Dolly Varden pond. That evening in the dining hall, George Prater remarked casually: "I went fishing up at the pond today. The scenery was sure good up there!"

On another occasion almost the whole cannery crew decided to try to hike around the lake. It was another of those off-the-wall, not-very-well-thought-out ideas we were full of. The lake was about ten miles long and had no trails to follow. We had to just climb along the shore, sometimes clinging to grass clumps and tree roots as we negotiated steep shores.

I was climbing along one of these steep rocky cliffs when the dog Molly came charging out of the woods. She was big, furry, and black, and I thought she was a bear. I let out a shriek and almost fell in, to everyone's immense enjoyment.

After that we decided that it would be all we could manage just to return the way we had come. When we got to the creek where the falls began, the water was running so swiftly we had to form a "human chain" on a rope to keep from being swept down the waterfall. Georgie Prater, the boss' son, was wearing his swimsuit and lost the bundle with his shirt, pants, and shoes down the falls. We pulled Molly the dog across by the rope.

Another adventurous jaunt was a trip in a skiff and kicker into the next bay where there was a salt lagoon. The fisherman who took us was thoroughly familiar with it, and pointed out that the lagoon filled when the tide was coming in, and the water flowed pretty fast into the lagoon. When the tide was going out, the water flooded just as fast in the other direction, so we needed to catch either high or low water slack to get into the lagoon. Unfortunately, we chose high water slack and got in very easily, but when we tried to go out we couldn't buck the current coming in and had to wait a number of hours for the water to slow down. But during that delightful afternoon we gazed in wonder at the shrimp, sea cucumbers, spiny sea urchins, and other weird critters on the bottom. I had never seen any of these in their native habitat before.

Frequently we would go on one of the tenders up into College Fiord where over 25 glaciers tumbled into the sea and could all be seen at once from the middle of the fiord. Here we gathered small icebergs for making ice cream or for keeping the fishermen's beer cold. Roy Hansen talked me into posing in my swimsuit on an iceberg while he took a picture.

It was another summer of too much time on our hands and not enough fish to keep us working and out of mischief. On an idle day one of the boats, flying a pirate flag as a gag, proposed that we all go over and visit Whittier.

Whittier was a new town, an Army base built during World War II, and none of us on the floater had seen it. We were anxious to go, and there seemed to be no fish in the cannery nor any en route aboard any tenders, so we just got on the boats and went. That was a mistake. We certainly should have consulted George Prater first, but we were young, idle and headstrong.

*Boats tied up during closed periods. The fishermen came onto the floater to visit and take showers.*

As we crossed Port Wells, where College Fiord emptied its icebergs and silty water, we were clowning around on deck, taking pictures and mugging for the camera. All three of us "6:30-ers" were aboard, and the two guys came up to me and said, "Let's jump overboard and catch the skiff!" The skiff was being towed behind the boat.

I thought this was a great idea, but made sure I told someone we were going over, just in case. Before they could stop us, we leaped in. The water was icy cold! You might say cold "like a glacier," but it was more like all 25 of those glaciers combined. When we bobbed to the surface, gasping from the sudden cold, the skiff had passed us. We were bobbing on this cold, milky green water and we could hear the skipper's voice swearing a blue streak. "G--Damn, what the H-- do they think they're doing?" and so on, while the boat wheeled around to pick us up.

I don't recall any bawling out or anything when we came aboard. I guess the skipper thought we learned enough from the frigidity of the water itself, or it could have been that my ears were too frozen to hear it.

We put into Whittier during the hot part of the day, climbing the high ladders up onto the Whittier dock. Since it was so warm, we hated to wear our hot cannery boots so we got the bright idea of going uptown barefoot. About 25 yards down the gravelly road we had figured out the flaw in this idea, but the boots were back on the boat by then. So we just limped along for a while.

Soon an Army truck came by and stopped in a cloud of dust. "You guys want a ride?" they asked. "Sure!" we all chorused, and climbed up onto the back of the truck, which took off once more in its dust cloud. We looked around and lo and behold, it was a garbage truck! Even so, none of our footsore crew wanted to get off. We just laughed about it—it would make a great story to tell at the end of the trip.

It didn't take very long to visit Whittier. It was still an Army camp and there really was nothing for us civilians except the PX, and we couldn't buy anything there. But we did enjoy it, and soon our "limousine" deposited us back at the dock.

The skipper of the boat said there was some construction work going on in nearby Pigot Bay, and we might want to see it. So we swung into this bay, and there we found a barge moored and a group of divers in hard suits and diving helmets working. We watched the work for a while and soon the guys knocked off for the evening. Since there were girls in

*Divers at Pigot Bay.*

the group visiting, they started up the phonograph and invited us to a dance there on the barge in the machine shop. They tried to tell us that "the guys aren't invited," but we brought them anyhow. They had to let the guys from our boat come or we wouldn't. The dance turned out to be fun and we had a great time. We departed late that night, with insincere invitations to come over and visit the floater "someday."

When we came around the point into Mink Bay I knew at once we were in trouble. There was steam up and they were canning fish. We hurried into our cannery clothes but Prater wouldn't let us work that shift, nor get paid for it. He was very angry with us, which we had to admit was justified. He maintained an icy silence around us for about two or three days.

Then one day he came in with a deck of cards in his hand and had everyone draw a card. He wanted to see who had the high and the low card. The high card drawer raised it up with a happy shout, "I got the ace!" and the low card person sheepishly showed his deuce. Prater then announced that they were both "Captains of the Head," and had won the right to clean the bathrooms. I could see he had been hoping that I had one or the other, as he knew I was one of the renegades responsible for the Whittier trip, but he didn't say anything. In fact, after that he returned to his normal good cheer. We, however, were a bit more subdued, at least for a little while.

But lo and behold, to our dismay the barge from Pigot Bay came waddling into Mink Bay on Saturday, complete with guys ready for a big dance and lots of fun.

George Prater met them and wouldn't let them tie up to the floater, sensing possible trouble. So they took their scow over to the middle of the bay and anchored there. They put on a diving exhibition for the local fishermen who were tied to the floater, and visited the fishermen aboard their boats with plenty of booze. Even those of us who had been to Pigot Bay could sense possible trouble, so we maintained an icy distance. We didn't want Prater mad at us, nor did we want any trouble aboard the floater or the boats alongside.

We ignored those guys, but they'd point us out and say "We know that one!" pointing to Angie or Marian or me, and we'd gaze off toward the mountains, as if we'd just seen a bear up there. Finally, after a day of visiting with the fishermen and not getting a chance to talk to any of the women, they pulled up the anchor and went back to Pigot Bay.

We usually clowned and danced a lot on the floating cannery with our own crew and the fishermen who fished for us and hardly ever had any kind of trouble; somehow this was different.

George Prater normally maintained a loose rein on his crew, allowing them to blow off steam as necessary. But when trouble was near, he had an instinct for it, and we tried to back him up in his efforts to avoid such trouble. He had gained our deepest respect. He was a good superintendent.

Meanwhile, my "Tom Sawyer" game went on, with the guys stitching boxes and my telling stories. The stitchery of the fishermen had greatly improved, and had almost filled the cannery warehouse full of boxes. The guys got to competing with each other, trying to make the fastest or the neatest stitches, and laughing at newer recruits whose stitches piled up on top of each other to maybe seven or eight staples deep.

Everyone knew what it was about. It was showing off for the pretty young floater girls. And for our part, we pretended to ignore the handsome young fishermen, full of lusty energy and adventurous spirit that really appealed to us. They were athletic, too, and more than once I had occasion to marvel at the lithe, agile grace of their movements around the boats. Working on a fishing boat really calls for such abilities.

As the season was winding down for the year, I was really sorry to leave the floater this time. Even the ritual extensions dragging out the fishing season didn't bother me so much. I had begun to figure it was all part of the fishing game or the 'war' or whatever it was. The potential future of the fisheries was hanging in the balance and the next few years would tell the story. There was nothing I could do about it, any more than the fishermen could. The fisheries couldn't go on forever like this, we all knew. The whole idea was to bring it to a head.

*Marian and friend horsing around on deck.*

# Chapter Twenty-Three

## HITCHHIKING ACROSS THE GULF
## PELICAN CITY

### September 1947

It was "after-season" time again; time to decide what to do next. Angie had met a very special fisherman, Fred Bennett, and was getting married. That left only the two of us "Wonder Girls," Marian and I. We were in town during the after-season bash and trying to come up with just one more "last fling."

Angie and I had recited our adventures hiking the Richardson to Marian, and I have a feeling that those stories had planted the seed of the next suggestion Marian came up with: "Let's hitchhike across the Gulf of Alaska on a fishing boat and see what Southeast Alaska has to offer!"

It wasn't hard to find such a fishing boat. Nearly the whole fleet was headed for Seattle, or at least some point further south at that time of year. We picked a boat with guys we knew and trusted, the Loyal. They had no objection to our riding along as they crossed the gulf.

We went back to the floater to get our duffel bags and my typewriter (by this time I had picked up a small manual typewriter somewhere and was making a try at writing about my experiences). I had left it on one of the dining hall tables while Marian and I went downtown. When I went into the room, I found a note in the typewriter. It said: "Even long-haired cooks can remain pure!"

I knew who was responsible. John Wiese, from the Fishermen's Union Hall, had been aboard the floater visiting with us when we discussed the trip. John thought it was very funny when we asked about it later.

The Loyal would sail in convoy with Altana and Valiant. It was always good to have help around in case of sudden storms or breakdowns. In the '40s a fishing boat would not be able to outrun an approaching storm. It would take several days to cross the Gulf, and we listened quite religiously for weather reports so we could pick our weather. It was still the "weather permitting" era.

*The Altana. One of the fishing boats making the run to Pelican after the 1947 fishing season.*

We were fortunate that the weather permitted the next day. It was a glorious day, bright and sunny. Marian and I fooled around on deck while the crew attended to various tasks, trips uptown and just getting ready in general. We played around on the Loyal, swinging in some ropes from the rigging, and now and then bearing a hand with the stowing of supplies and such. We were sorry Angie wasn't coming with us.

At last all was in readiness. The tide was right and the weather reports were right; the three boats left the Cordova harbor for the three-day crossing of the Gulf of Alaska. The water seemed calm enough when we started out. But as we rounded Hinchinbrook Entrance we entered a sea swell still rolling in after a storm that had passed. Before the first day was over, I was beginning to get very, very seasick. I was hanging onto the rigging and feeding fishes over the side when one of the crew, afraid I'd fall overboard, came over to hold me and prevent such an accident, but it wasn't necessary, as I had a grip of steel on the guy ropes.

He said to me, "Why are you so afraid?" As sick as I was, I thought that was a stupid question. I wasn't afraid—I was seasick! But I was too sick to discuss it so I let it pass. Finally I went to sleep in my bunk below.

When I woke the next morning, the swell was still with us, but the seasickness had passed. In fact, I was beginning to enjoy the motion of the sea. Over the years I have found that the first twelve hours or so is all it takes for me to get my "sea legs." After that I have little chance of seasickness again on the same voyage. I was feeling wobbly but well, and ate a cautious breakfast. Then I began to have a good time.

As with most fishing boats in those days, there was no "head" (toilet) aboard, so when necessity dictated, Marian or I would find a deck bucket and disappear into the fo'c'sle, close the door and take care of business. The Loyal was a big fishing boat for that era. Most boats did not have a separate fo'c'sle for sleeping. The guys, when necessity called, simply made a sign to us girls, and we'd disappear into the pilot-house for coffee so they could use the rail for the purpose.

Rinsing the bucket afterward was quite a trick, and both Marian and I had been coached carefully in the technique and in the danger of the process. The danger was that the bucket could easily pull you overboard before you could blink an eye or holler "Help!" The trick was to throw the bucket forward and NEVER let it get past yourself before dragging it up again. Many lives have been lost performing this one simple nautical maneuver, so I was not trusted to do it without someone holding me.

Marian had served in the Swedish Merchant Marine and could be trusted with this simple (but dangerous) duty, but not I. Even though I had been introduced to it on fishing boats, the skipper knew I was still a rookie, and his orders were firm: "Someone ALWAYS hold her while she rinses the bucket!"

I was thoroughly insulted, and though I protested, the skipper was adamant and would not change his mind—it was really that dangerous. The skipper said, "I don't give a damn what she says, someone hold her!" And of course his orders to me were: "Don't rinse the damn bucket without someone holding you!" The captain had spoken, and I had no recourse. I had to submit to this indignity.

Marian and I exchanged jokes about the mystique of "head-less" fishing boats, deck buckets and rails. Marian designed a certificate, complete with what passed for gold-leaf filigree around the edges ("scrambled eggs" in the military). It proclaimed our charter membership into "THE DECK BUCKET AND RAIL CLUB," a very exclusive club indeed.

*Lone E. Janson*

The seas continued high, but the seasickness had passed, and it didn't bother me again. We were all out on deck enjoying the sunshine, visiting, and drinking bottles of beer. One time we ran out of beer, so one of the guys got on the radio to the Altana and asked if they had any more beer. Since they did, they dropped back and fairly close alongside, where they threw us a rope. Then they tied bottles of beer to the rope and proceeded to re-supply our vessel.

I think it was the third day when we finally reached Cross Sound, the entrance to Southeast Alaska. As soon as we entered the sound, we turned to starboard and headed down a narrow channel to Pelican City, our destination.

Pelican City had no cars at all and no roads, only sidewalks built on stilts, a different version of the familiar wooden sidewalks of early Alaska. Where the walks were over water, they were lined with picket fences.

Pelican City was strictly a cannery town. We landed there on a Saturday, so the cannery would be showing movies that evening in their warehouse. I watched the movie from a very comfortable crossbeam high up in the ceiling of the warehouse. I thought of it as exclusive loge seating.

After the movie, Marian and I and the crewmen of the boats in our convoy went down the resounding boardwalks to a little bar where they were throwing a dance. It was a close-knit crowd, all fishing types, so the atmosphere was just right for another of those crazy, off-the-wall dances. My shoes were ratty and ready to fall apart, so I suggested we all dance barefoot. It seems that such oddball suggestions were snapped up by roistering crowds in those days, so we all threw our shoes in the corner of the dancehall and danced the night away.

When it was time to head for the boat again, I dug through the pile for my shoes, but only found one. The other had vanished. We started back down to the boat, and I decided that one shoe was of no use to me, so I tossed it over the picket fence into the water. The next morning as I made my way uptown along the boardwalk in a pair of cannery boots, I found the other shoe stuck on one of the pickets where I would be sure to find it! For the next month or so I had to carry my good luck penny in my cannery boots.

Marian and I were looking around for a deckhand job on a fishing boat, and we found one on a small, unnamed boat that simply bore a cannery designation and number. The skipper's name was Harold, and the other deck hand was Johnny. We would be out only a few weeks for the Silver salmon season. The skipper told us to tell other fishermen we were going to Dry Bay, but our actual destination was Lituya Bay, a very historic, tiny T-shaped bay off the Gulf of Alaska, only seven miles long and about a mile or so wide.

*Lone E. Janson*

# Chapter Twenty-Four

## LITUYA BAY

### September 1947

Our voyage across the Gulf to Lituya Bay was spectacular beyond belief. We had chosen our weather well. It was clear, cloudless and sunny. The Gulf of Alaska was in one of its rare calm moods. The mountains on our right rose majestically from the sea to incredible heights. On our left the great ocean stretched to the horizon and we could only sense the distances beyond.

Outside the entrance of the bay we hove to, waiting for dead slack high water. The entrance to Lituya Bay was only 33 feet deep, and the tide poured through with deadly fury, creating vicious whirlpools. It was only at high water slack, as the tide paused and prepared to turn and head the other way, that there was a short respite when the water calmed and boats could safely enter.

This was a calm day and its deceptive quietness did not alert me to the evidence of mighty forces at hand. The area had the same verdant beauty I had seen in Southeast Alaska and Prince William Sound. Here was the same scenic quality I had known on the floating cannery, except for the nearness and height of the mountains beyond. Marian and I sat on the pilothouse with the skipper waiting for the magic interval when we could enter. I felt the lure of mysterious but deadly beauty. There was a siren quality about the place: alluring but menacing too. It was so quiet out here today. But what was that small sibilant growl of warning? Was it just the quieted surf?

Lituya Bay truly fulfilled the yearning for adventure that had brought me to Alaska. This was one of the far, forgotten, isolated places that was so wild, beautiful and forbidding that it satisfied every idea I had of the offbeat and unusual. Lituya Bay is located right on the Fairweather Fault, home of the strongest earthquakes on this continent. Lituya Bay is possibly the most unpredictable and violent place on this planet. Here several tectonic plates of the earth constantly carry on a gargantuan battle as one slips beneath the other, creating those great mountains.

*Lone E. Janson*

As a result of these forces, Lituya Bay has a long history of gigantic, seismic-generated tidal waves, some reaching thousands of feet high up on the mountainside, where entire forests have been scoured away by their force. Only the sparseness of population accounts for the few lives lost. Some time after we fished there, one of these waves caught three fishing boats inside, sinking two instantly and washing the third clear over La Chaussee Spit into the Gulf of Alaska. All persons on the first two boats perished, but all on the third survived.

Even before we approached the entrance to this tiny bay, I sensed the tenseness of the captain. His chubby face was serious, his pale blue eyes watchful. He studied his tide tables with extra care and searched the sky for weather portents.

I surveyed the scene. To one side was a long spit, named La Chaussee Spit by La Perouse, who discovered the bay in 1789. On the other side were two small perfectly shaped, cone-like outcrops, called The Paps. Beyond lay the majestic heights of the St. Elias Mountains, and such mountains they were!

Lituya Bay was only seven miles long, with two glaciers at the head, forming a "T" shape, right on the Fault line.

*Taken in Lituya Bay.*

We lay offshore at what looked like a long distance. The ocean all along the Gulf of Alaska maintains a constant roaring of waves washing against the shore. On calm days, such as this, it is a mere whisper. On windy days it is a mighty crescendo of surf against sandy shore. So I listened as we waited and thought I could hear the whirlpools, but I could not be sure.

When the tide was right, we sailed peacefully inside with no evidence of the deadly whirlpools. Then we could really see the height and steepness of the mountains, and the beautiful island in the middle of the bay, called Cenotaph Island. During La Perouse's time in Lituya Bay, twenty-one of his men had been swept into the entrance whirlpools and drowned. He erected a cenotaph, or monument, on the island in their honor.

It was Harold, the skipper, who told us this story, as he had read a bit of the history of Lituya Bay.

"That monument has never been found," he mused. "It would be worth a fortune to anyone who found it." He had no description of it. He said, "If it was made of wood, I don't think anyone will ever find it. If it was made of stone or something else, maybe."

Cenotaph Island had a steep bird rookery off the eastern end, and the cliff-dwelling birds made a cacophony of sound and fury when we approached that end of the island. The island had been home to a blue fox farm at one stage in its history, but the problem encountered by the fox farmer was that there was no source of good water on the island, and he had to constantly import water for his charges.

One of the most memorable things about the island was the abundance of berries. We went ashore with buckets to pick blueberries one day, and I filled a very large bucket with fat, juicy blueberries from just one small bush! The bush looked like a blue fountain before I started picking. I was too much a rookie sourdough to recognize this abundance of berries reflected the absence of bears.

We took a number of trips to the head of the bay, where the icebergs calving off the glaciers sounded like distant cannon fire. Seals lounged comfortably on the icebergs from the glaciers, hitting the water with a splash as soon as we approached.

We were there to gather ice, and Johnny came to the bow with a long pike pole in hand while the skipper brought us up alongside a small berg. I wondered why he was fooling with such a small chunk when there were plenty of larger ones around, but when Johnny tried to pull this one aboard, we saw that it was too large! I forgot how much of the iceberg is below the water. We had to look around for ones that looked hardly bigger than ice cubes to haul them aboard.

From there we went down past Cenotaph Island and set our gillnets near a small stream off to the side of the bay. When the Silvers were picked from the nets, we gutted and cleaned them and packed them in crushed glacier ice.

This was different from the custom in Prince William Sound, where tenders constantly picked up the fresh fish from the fishermen without the necessity of pre-cleaning and icing. Icing down was new to me. When we were in Pelican City, I overheard one of the fishermen, a trawler who customarily fished in the outside waters of the Gulf, complaining because he couldn't get cured ice until the next day. There was plenty of ice at the cannery, he said, but it was not yet properly cured. When I asked him about it, he explained that ordinary ice from an icemaker would not hold fish because it melted too soon—it was not cold enough. Ice had to be cured for a certain amount of time before they could use it.

Glacier ice was superior to the cured ice at the cannery. Glacier ice, being compacted snow (as opposed to frozen water), melts much more slowly than other ice. Glacier ice was often served in bar drinks in certain areas where it was readily available. In Lituya Bay we had a ready source of glacier ice for our fish, and also to keep our beer cold.

Meanwhile, Harold told us of the nearby beaches where ruby sand could be found. "Ruby sand is usually a sign of placer gold in the sand, too," he remarked. We decided to take a hike over the meadows to the ocean beach and look for ruby sand on the next weekend.

The next Saturday was a perfect day for a hike and picnic. As we started hiking across a grassy meadow of the island, I stumbled on a rock or something in the deep grass. There was definitely something solid there. My mind immediately went to the missing cenotaph, and as I brushed the dead grasses away from this rock, or whatever, it appeared as something man-made, something of cement. I let out a big yelp.

"It's the cenotaph!" I declared, feverishly scratching more and more tangled grass away from the small monument that was there. Everyone gathered around me as I finally cleared it, and found a small brass plate on the base. It read "U.S. Coast and Geodetic Survey." Inasmuch as La Perouse was here in the late 1700's, I figured it really couldn't be the missing cenotaph after all, but it really was a cenotaph! My shipmates had a hearty laugh at my expense over that one.

We did find ruby sand on the beach. Harold was slightly color-blind, and since red was one color he had trouble seeing, he had a hard time seeing the tiny rubies in ruby sand. It appeared to him as darker sand, so he wanted us to confirm whether it was truly ruby sand or not. It was. We had no gold pan, so did not try to pan any out, but Harold said that the sand must have come from under the many glaciers up in the St. Elias Mountains, and that under those glaciers must be a treasure trove of gold.

We ate our small picnic lunch here on the beach and hiked back, still speculating on the wealth of gold under the St. Elias glaciers, seemingly so near at hand. On the high peaks lay new snow, "termination dust," again. Winter was getting close, and I would soon have to figure out how and where to spend my winter.

We returned to fishing. I was getting my first taste of drift gillnetting and learning how to pick fish out of the net. Everything was new to me. Even on the floater I had never had a chance to try the fishing I saw the men do every day. Now I learned how to actually handle the big, beautiful salmon we caught and how to clear the web from the gills.

I was also getting a feel for life aboard a fishing boat, and although the living quarters were cramped and often damp, I found the experience stimulating and rich in new and unexpected rewards. There was the seagull that was so tame he would come right onto the boat as we cleaned and iced the fish, accepting tidbits hand-fed to him by the skipper. One morning we woke up to see a black cormorant perched on the stern, and even though he was not as comfortable with humans as the seagull, he still was an enchanting visitor. Seals and porpoises abounded in the bay. I was beginning to think I might like this fisherman's life. It was rough and tough and, well, wonderful.

Although fishing life had its rewards and was rich in life-quality, we were not exactly netting much money. In fact, our season was very poor. We made just about enough to pay our share of the groceries and nothing more. We were still at the anchorage inside Lituya Bay, finishing icing the fish and other chores to get ready to go back to Pelican City. We knew how many fish we had, so we went ahead with settling up.

Fishermen were paid by shares: so much for the boat, so much for the skipper, and the rest divided among the crew. But before the shares were counted, all of us split the cost of the ship's stores, and at the end of the season any leftover canned goods were divided among the crew.

We had virtually no money coming, and since we didn't want to carry them around with us, we gave our share of what was left of the ship's stores to Johnny and Harold. The sheer adventure of Lituya Bay had been enough reward, but, as they say, it "makes thin soup."

Of course, we knew how it worked when we signed on. If the season was a bust, we went busted too. If it was good, we got good pay. It was just part of the game, but I was beginning to foresee some dinners of "rabbit tracks and snowballs" coming up this winter.

Even though the outlook for winter was a little doubtful at this point, I had been through enough to feel confident that I could deal with anything the future might throw at me. After all, I had a penny in my shoe for luck, didn't I?

I hadn't forgotten my dream of writing about Alaska. I cast a longing glance to where my small portable typewriter was stowed under a bunk, not touched at all during the season's fishing. I needed a place to bring it out and set it up somewhere. By now I had plenty of Alaskan adventures to write about.

*A Cormorant on the stern of the boat.*

*Lone E. Janson*

# Chapter Twenty-Five

## SO YOU'LL NEVER GO BROKE
### October 1947

Once more we waited for high water slack, and said our adieus to famous old Lituya Bay. As we sailed out of the entrance to Lituya Bay and headed across the Gulf of Alaska to Cross Sound, I began to wonder what the winter would hold for me in Southeast Alaska.

I considered the coming winter and my limited funds, and I began to feel a bit blue about our failure in the fishing season. For much of the trip I sat in the door to the pilothouse watching the tremendous waves of Cross Sound and considering my future and my past two years in Alaska.

Cross Sound is noted for high swells as currents from the protected waters of Southeast Alaska fight at cross-purposes with the currents and swells from the Gulf of Alaska. I was beginning to appreciate what this meant as we approached the area.

On this final crossing I saw the largest waves I had ever encountered. They were huge, maybe a hundred feet or more from bottom to top, although the day was calm and clear with hardly any wind. The waves were not breaking; they just mounted higher and higher as we slid to the bottom of one set, only to be lifted in a smooth gradual glide to the top of the next and slide gently down the other side. They didn't strike terror into me, but they certainly were awe-inspiring.

As I watched those mountainous swells build up, gradually raise the boat to their heights and bring it down again, I tried to decide what to do now that the season was over.

I thought back on all my Alaskan adventures since I arrived here two years ago. I could not have imagined the nature of the adventures that awaited me, but they had fulfilled every dream of adventure I had ever dreamed. Well, I reflected, that's what adventure is—something you never expected.

There was the one-armed "Good Samaritan," whose non-judgmental kindness taught me not to feel sorry for myself. There was Ma Pullen's Skagway and White Pass and the Glacier Section House where I learned about cold storage eggs and "Klim." There was the Alcan Highway, where I saw how big-huge-awesome-empty this thing called "Wilderness" can be. There was winter in Fairbanks—and then summer in Fairbanks. The Richardson Highway: by bus or by thumb, that pioneer road was a "far piece" from anything I had ever encountered. Esther Island with its magnificent waterfall setting was the ultimate experience and adventure both years. Then there was the Alaska Railroad and its incredible "loop," and Alaska Nellie, and finally Nome! Nome, where because of the midnight sun, you could look right into tomorrow. I had seen Juneau, Pelican City, and mysterious and powerful places like Lituya Bay.

I even wrote an unfinished piece of doggerel verse about it:

*"From the rugged peaks of Skagway*
*To the sandy Bering's shore,*
*On far, forgotten islands*
*Where mountain torrents roar..."*

I tried to add more, but never got any further. Still I liked the few lines I had written. I certainly had piled up an impressive array of exotic experiences and impressions of a fleetingly brief time in history.

My experience on the fishing boat in Lituya Bay had felt like a way of life that I could get used to. For that reason, I began toying with the idea of settling in a fishing community, and the community I knew best was Cordova. Aside from the rich and diverse history of the area and the adventurous fishing lifestyle, I had made many good friends who lived there.

I thought back many times to the skiff rides with Roy Hansen, the seal hunt, the trips to Katalla to visit his dad, the old engine abandoned on the doorstep of Bering Glacier, and the site of the old Chilkat village on Bering River. Roy epitomized the very roots of Alaska; he practically grew up on a fishing boat, and his life had been subsistence hunting and trapping, combined with commercial fishing. He was a Tlingit Indian, and my first buddies, the "Mad Hansens" were his sisters. They were still there, in Cordova, while my wonderful friends, Juli, Angie, and Marian, had all peeled off to pursue their own lives. I would miss them, I knew. But I could still go back to Cordova and the whole

Hansen tribe would be there to welcome me.

I knew then that I would not go back "Down Below" for this winter, but I had to go somewhere. I knew that in Cordova there were still a few weeks of crab cannery work available. I liked the place, and I felt more at home there than anywhere I had been in Alaska.

I had the feeling that it was time for a change in my life. But what kind of change? I wasn't sure. But I remembered that little manual typewriter down under the forward bunk. I thought if I could just find a place where I could pull it out, I could begin writing. Then it would all come together.

I had tried to write stories ever since I was a little kid barely able to string words together. All my life I had been trying to write, but it seemed I never knew what to write about. I had felt too young and naive, with nothing worthwhile to say. Now I had a lot of things to write about but no place to do it. But at least I had a typewriter, which was a lot like having a boat to go fishing in.

The people of Alaska, what a strange mix they were. They accepted me, just as I was. They thought I was crazy but it was their own brand of craziness, so I fit right in. They prized individualism, they abhorred being forced into molds that "civilization" had created for them, but they had a few "molds" of their own, like their penchant for getting young women "hitched." There were friends everywhere, and loneliness everywhere. There were "miles and miles of miles and miles" with no one at all in them. There was even my fancied sixty square miles for one unmarried female!

Wandering around was fun, and had fulfilled something inside me that needed fulfillment. But now I needed a place where I could sit still for a winter and pull out my typewriter to write. I knew what my subject was—Alaska!

I thought about the stories I had heard about the longshore strike last winter, which I had come to think of as the "Winter of Siege." I wanted to be with my friends if something like that happened again. I didn't want to be a thousand miles away wondering how they were. So it was that I decided I would go back to Cordova. I felt I belonged in Cordova now.

Our little boat had passed the great waves of Cross Sound, and after a short voyage we put into Juneau boat harbor, where "Fishface Sam's" place was still in business. Marian met her beau and they departed for a wedding and Marian's future.

I boarded the next Alaska Steamship for Cordova. By some odd circumstance, it was Alaska Steamship's *Cordova* that took me back to the town where I would spend the next thirty years.

When I docked at Cordova, the "Mad Hansens" and many of their clan, including Roy, were there on the dock, just as I anticipated. They were genuinely happy to welcome me back, and I felt totally at home.

I rented a room at the Windsor Hotel, where I had first stayed in Cordova, and as soon as I could arrange it, I made a long distance call to my mother.

I told her of my latest adventures and that I would be wintering in Cordova. We visited for a while, then as an afterthought I asked: "Mom, you know how you used to tell me that when you were bumming around the country you should always wear a penny in your shoe? Why was that?"

Mom's musical laughter rang back along the telephone wire. "Why, honey," she said, "I thought you knew! It's an old custom from Depression days. It's so you'll never go broke!!"

And in over 60 years living and writing in Alaska, I never really have.

# Epilogue

## KIDNAPPED BY A BOOK

Writing on my book began that very fall, 1947, when I got back to Cordova. I dug out my journals and began typing as soon as I found a table for my typewriter.

That's the book I started, but that wasn't the one that got written first. Instead, the book that took over my life in Cordova was to emerge eventually as "The Copper Spike," the story of the building of the Copper River & Northwestern Railway from Cordova to Kennecott, a story that included some places I had already seen: Cordova, Katalla and Bering River.

In November 1947, I married Roy Hansen, and we spent that first winter in Katalla, the same "ghost town" we had explored during the last summer from the floater. Roy was trapping there, along with five or six other trapping families. We lived with his dad, old Bill Hansen, because there were no other live-able houses left in Katalla. There were many old buildings remaining from Katalla's heyday—the school, the business buildings, some homes, and even the old hotel where Wiley Post had stayed during his round-the-world flight. Fascinating as these old structures were, they were all crumbling under the effects of time, salt sea air, and rain.

You could not be in that ghost town of Katalla more than two days without running into "the railroad story" everywhere you turned. Aside from the overgrown railroad tracks, there were the stories of events still remembered by people living in the ruins of what had once been a prosperous town.

People told about the great storms of autumn, and showed me where the old breakwater was supposed to be. They pointed out Palm Point, the terminus of another smaller railroad. From a distance the shattered tops of tall spruce trees looked just like palm trees. I saw the foundations of old oil wells along Katalla Slough, where rhubarb plants grew instead of nettles.

*Lone with Roy Hansen, her first husband, shortly after they were married in November 1947.*

Somewhere out in the woods were the remains of the oil refinery that had burned on Christmas Day 1933.

I remember very well the old engine "Ole" on Bering River Flats, which was part of the story. That winter we walked the overgrown right-of-way that led toward Bering Lake and the coalfields beyond—coalfields that Washington D.C. bureaucrats had closed down. People even showed me pictures of old Katalla buildings with signs in the windows: "Closed. Killed by Conservation." There was a story here, but what exactly was it? No one had the whole story, only bits and pieces of it.

There was unwritten history all around me, and I have to admit that the siren song had begun to play in my head. But I still didn't know what was happening—that I was being kidnapped by a book crying to be written.

Discovering what had happened here was a mystery that would take more than twenty years of frustrating research. During all those years of research and writing, I was working in the summers either in a cannery or aboard the fishing boat, making a living. So I would find myself in some isolated cannery in the evenings, sitting with my little Smith-Corona, typing away. During the fishing season, at breaks I could be found in the cabin below perched on the edge of a bunk, turned sort of sideways so I could reach the keys of that little manual typewriter on the let-down table. My research materials and extra paper were in big heavy boxes stowed under the forward bunk along with the spare anchor.

On our return to Cordova, I found many signs of the old railroad still there. The canneries called us to work with a railroad train whistle, that lonesome "Whoo-oo-ee" sound, different from any other. Songs have been written about that "Lonesome whistle, blowin' down the trestle..." It's very distinctive and calls up all sorts of memories to old-timers. I walked along the "lower road" which was the old railroad track, on my way to the cannery, reflecting on how ties were always the wrong distance apart for a comfortable walking step.

I heard people talk of the old roundhouse that had stood in Cordova's "old town" for years after the railroad stopped running. I had not seen it before it was destroyed by fire, but one of the railroad warehouses that had stood nearby still marked the spot.

That winter after Katalla, I began to run into more old-timers who remembered railroad stories about Cordova. They would pull me aside and tell me these great yarns and I'd scribble notes as fast as I could on the back of some old envelope or on a cocktail napkin or whatever I could find. After a while other old-timers began searching me out to tell their stories.

At that time I didn't even know I was writing "The Copper Spike." After I got a few good railroad tales, I decided they'd make a great article for the "Alaska Sportsman," the only market for Alaskan stories that there was. Magazines on the "Outside" didn't want Alaskan stories—at

*Lone E. Janson*

least not true ones. They might consider Jack London macho-type fiction, but the real Alaska was taboo.

I began the "Alaska Sportsman" article, figuring that all I needed to weave the stories together was a little background on the railroad so it all fit together logically. So I went to the library.

The Cordova library at that time consisted of a small room run by a volunteer, open a couple of days a week and stocked with mostly paperback novels. They were for winter reading, not research. After all, Cordova was a fairly large town in the summer, when the "Outside" fishermen arrived from Seattle, Ballard and Westport. But in the winter, when only the real Alaskans stayed, it was very small. We used to say that Cordova's major export was fish, and its major import was fishermen!

With no background on the railroad, the article I was trying to write was foiled. I simply couldn't find ANY HISTORY at all about the defunct Copper River & Northwestern Railway.

The years passed and somehow the small tidbits of information gradually piled up. I gathered them all and tucked them away like a busy little squirrel. By this time I had discovered a few mysteries from obscure sources. One book mentioned a "fake town site," but didn't bother to explain anything more about it. On another occasion I found a sentence about a "gun battle," but no hint of where this happened or any of the circumstances surrounding it. I felt like I was holding a tiger by the tail—you can't hang on, but you really can't let go either!

By now I was married a second time, to another Tlingit fisherman who lived in Cordova, Dick Janson Jr. Dick had first noticed me when he'd thrown me overboard for a dollar years earlier!

He encouraged me to continue working against all odds on the railroad story. By this time I had stories from BOTH of my fathers-in-law, Bill Hansen and Dick Janson Sr., both of whom I dearly loved, and from my sister-in-law Stella Janson.

My husband, Dick Jr., was secretary for the local fishermen's union, and we went to Seattle each fall to man a satellite office for the Cordova fishermen's union. So I had a chance to explore a few more libraries in bigger towns.

To my surprise, there was nothing there either. In desperation, I made up my mind to do a fiction story about it. I began this great

*Dick & Lone Janson*

blood-and-thunder novel outline, and I sent a copy of the outline to Dick's dad. Old Dick wrote back and informed me that book had already been written. "You need to read Rex Beach's novel 'The Iron Trail,'" he wrote.

So there I was again. Stymied. It was about this time it dawned on me that this history had never been written! When that realization sank in, I suddenly recognized the tremendous opportunity it offered me. I'd be the first!

This was a book crying out to be written! Well, I certainly wanted to, if only I could find the full story, the documentation, and the background. I already had the important part, the first-hand stories of all these people that knew the story so well. But none of them were in a position to know the whole story, a fact that made the riddle more puzzling.

The more I dug up, the more complex the story became. In this epic, everyone got into the act—the politicians, the greedy capitalists,

*Lone E. Janson*

the eq                                            aking journalists, the Native people, and the small coal miners who bore the brunt of the whole thing.

It involved oil, coal, copper, Native rights, and cutthroat railroad competition in the old "Union Pacific" tradition. It even affected the outcome of a Presidential election. No wonder no one knew the whole story!

I have never been a great believer in Fate, but perhaps I was the only one stubborn enough to just keep after it for over twenty years. In 1967 my first book "The Copper Spike" was published at last.

And now, sixty years later, I have finished the book I started so long ago. I never left my Alaska home, and after all these years I know that penny in my shoe without a doubt brought me luck!